Python Interviews

Discussions with Python Experts

Mike Driscoll

BIRMINGHAM - MUMBAI

PYTHON INTERVIEWS

Copyright © 2018 Packt Publishing

All rights reserved. No part of this book may be reproduced, stored in a retrieval system, or transmitted in any form or by any means, without the prior written permission of the publisher, except in the case of brief quotations embedded in critical articles or reviews.

Every effort has been made in the preparation of this book to ensure the accuracy of the information presented. However, the information contained in this book is sold without warranty, either express or implied. Neither the author, nor Packt Publishing or its dealers and distributors, will be held liable for any damages caused or alleged to have been caused directly or indirectly by this book.

Packt Publishing has endeavored to provide trademark information about all of the companies and products mentioned in this book by the appropriate use of capitals. However, Packt Publishing cannot guarantee the accuracy of this information.

Acquisition Editor: Ben Renow-Clarke
Project Editor: Radhika Atitkar
Content Development Editors: Joanne Lovell
Technical Editor: Gaurav Gavas
Copy Editor: Joanne Lovell
Indexer: Tejal Daruwale Soni
Graphics: Tom Scaria
Production Coordinator: Arvindkumar Gupta

First published: February 2018

Production reference: 2290318

Published by Packt Publishing Ltd.
Livery Place
35 Livery Street
Birmingham B3 2PB, UK.
ISBN 978-1-78839-908-1

www.packtpub.com

"Python" and the Python Logo are trademarks of the Python Software Foundation.

mapt.io

Mapt is an online digital library that gives you full access to over 5,000 books and videos, as well as industry leading tools to help you plan your personal development and advance your career. For more information, please visit our website.

Why subscribe?

- Spend less time learning and more time coding with practical eBooks and Videos from over 4,000 industry professionals
- Learn better with Skill Plans built especially for you
- Get a free eBook or video every month
- Mapt is fully searchable
- Copy and paste, print, and bookmark content

PacktPub.com

Did you know that Packt offers eBook versions of every book published, with PDF and ePub files available? You can upgrade to the eBook version at www.PacktPub.com and as a print book customer, you are entitled to a discount on the eBook copy. Get in touch with us at service@packtpub.com for more details.

At www.PacktPub.com, you can also read a collection of free technical articles, sign up for a range of free newsletters, and receive exclusive discounts and offers on Packt books and eBooks.

FOREWORD

Welcome, all, to *Python Interviews*!

People often get confused about open source programming languages, focusing merely on the technology behind the language — be it the language itself, the libraries available for it, or the impressive products that are built with it — and not on the ecosystem of individuals that are responsible for the language existing in the first place.

Python is an open source language, driven mostly by volunteer efforts from all around the globe. It's important to focus not only on the technology behind what makes Python great, but also the individuals that make it great as well.

The world of Python is not one comprised merely of code, but of a community of like-minded individuals coming together to make the world a better place through the open source ethos. Thousands of individuals have contributed towards the success of Python.

This book contains interviews with an excellent selection of the individuals that power Python and its wonderful open source community. It dives into the personal backgrounds of these individuals and the opinions they have about the community, the technology, and the direction we're headed in, together.

But, must importantly — it exposes that Python, the programing language, is indeed comprised of persons, just like you, trying to make a difference in the world, one step at a time.

Kenneth Reitz

Director at Large for the Python Software Foundation

CONTRIBUTOR

About the Author

Mike Driscoll has been using Python since April 2006. He blogs for the Python Software Foundation. Other than blogging, he enjoys reading novels, listening to a wide variety of music, and learning photography. He writes documentation for the wxPython project's wiki page and helps wxPython users on their mailing list. He also helps Python users on the PyWin32 list and occasionally the comp.lang.py list too.

Packt is Searching for Authors Like You

If you're interested in becoming an author for Packt, please visit `authors.packtpub.com` and apply today. We have worked with thousands of developers and tech professionals, just like you, to help them share their insight with the global tech community. You can make a general application, apply for a specific hot topic that we are recruiting an author for, or submit your own idea.

TABLE OF CONTENTS

PREFACE

Near the end of 2016, I was brainstorming with my editor about the kinds of books might be of interest. I had been doing a series of articles on my blog called *PyDev of the Week* that inspired us into crafting a book based on interviewing core members of the Python community. I spent some time hashing out 20 names of people that I thought would be good for the book and then I started contacting them in 2017.

Over the course of about 8-12 months, I ended up interviewing 20 pillars of the Python community, although my list changed several times over that period. Some people weren't available or couldn't be reached. But I persevered and managed to pull together a well-rounded set of representatives of the Python programming community.

In this book, you will get interesting anecdotes about the history of Python and its creators, such as Brett Cannon and Nick Coghlan. You will discover why Python didn't have Unicode support in its first release, and you'll hear from core developers about where they think Python is going in the future. You will also hear from some well-known Python authors, like Al Sweigart, Luciano Ramalho, and Doug Hellman.

I also spoke with some of the creators or core developers of popular third-party packages in Python, such as web2py (Massimo Di Pierro), SQLAlchemy (Mike Bayer), and the Twisted Framework (Glyph Lefkowitz), among others.

My interview with Carol Willing was a lot of fun. She is also a core developer of the Python language itself, so learning her views on women in technology and Python was quite enlightening. She is also a contributor to Project Jupyter, so learning more about that project was exciting.

I think you will find Alex Martelli and Steve Holden's interviews to be especially compelling as they have been working with Python for a very long time and have many interesting insights.

There is a lot to learn from all the individuals that I spoke with. If you happen to know them, you know that even better than I do. All of them were great to chat with and very responsive to me even on the shortest of timelines. If you happen to meet them at a conference, be sure to thank them for their contributions.

Special thanks go out to all the people I interviewed. They took time out of their lives to help me with this project and I truly appreciate it. I also want to thank my editors for keeping this project on track. Finally, I would like to thank my wife, Evangeline, for putting up with me interviewing people at random times throughout the summer. And finally, I want to thank you, dear reader, for checking out this book.

1

Brett Cannon

Brett Cannon is a Canadian software engineer and Python core developer. He is a principal software developer at Microsoft, where he works on editing tools. Previous roles include software engineer at Google and creator at Oplop. Brett became a fellow of the Python Software Foundation (PSF) in 2003 and served as a director of the PSF between 2013 and 2014. He is a former PyCon US committee member and was conference chair of PyData Seattle 2017. Brett led the migration of CPython to GitHub and created `importlib`. Among his open source achievements is *caniusepython3* and he is the co-author of *17 successful Python Enhancement Proposals.*

Discussion themes: core developers, v2.7/v3.x, Python sprints.
Catch up with Brett Cannon here: @brettsky

Mike Driscoll: Why did you become a computer programmer?

Brett Cannon: I always found computers interesting, as far back as I can remember. I was lucky enough to go to an elementary school with a computer lab full of Apple IIes, back when that was the cutting edge, so I was exposed to them relatively early on.

In the year between junior high and high school, I took a computer class over the summer and that included a little bit of Apple BASIC. I did it and I excelled at it, to the point that I think I finished the entire class in the first week. It hadn't really clicked that I could do that for a job at that point.

This continued through high school, and then when it came time to pick courses for junior college, my mom had me promise her two things. I agreed that I would take a course in philosophy and I would take a course in computer programming. So that's what I did and I loved both.

Once again, I read my introductory C book in the first two weeks, which was supposed to last for the whole semester. I remember the first time I finished it, I sat down and implemented tic-tac-toe one day after class. I even forgot to eat dinner! It was just one of those eureka moments. The feeling of boundless creativity that this tool provided just engulfed me. That's how I got into programming.

> **Brett Cannon: 'The feeling of boundless creativity that this tool provided just engulfed me. That's how I got into programming.'**

I knew that tic-tac-toe was a solved problem, so I thought that I could actually write the logic so that I could play tic-tac-toe perfectly as a program. I spent something like six hours one evening doing it, and I was utterly blown away that I was actually able to do that. It opened up the possibilities of what computers could do, and the freedom of it and the ability to think about the problems just really grabbed me. I've been doing it ever since.

Driscoll: What led you to becoming so involved with Python and its community?

Cannon: Well, I ended up going to Berkeley and getting a degree in philosophy, but I kept taking computer science courses. The introductory computer science course at Berkeley had an entrance exam, and I was worried that I didn't know object-oriented programming, since I only knew C. So I looked around for an object-oriented programming language. I found Python, learned it, loved it, and kept writing personal programs in it.

At some point along the way, I needed `time.strptime`, the function to take a string that represents a `datetime` and parse it back into a time tuple. I was on Windows at the time, and `time.strptime` wasn't available on Windows. As a result, I came up with a way to parse it where you had to still plug in the locale information but it would still parse it.

Back then, ActiveState's cookbook site was still a thing, so I posted my recipe of how to do `strptime` up on ActiveState. Later, O'Reilly published the first edition of *Python Cookbook*, and Alex Martelli included that recipe as the last recipe in the book, which also happened to be the longest recipe in the book.

> **Brett Cannon: 'So I posted my recipe of how to do strptime up on ActiveState.'**

It still ticked me off, though, that people had to input their locale information. I was frustrated that I couldn't solve that. So in the back of my mind, I was continuously thinking about how I could get that locale information out. Eventually, I solved it. It was actually the week after graduating from Berkeley, and I gifted myself the time to write up the solution, so that you didn't have to enter locale information anymore.

After I did that, I emailed Alex Martelli, since we'd exchanged emails a couple of times at that point, and I said, "Hey, I've fixed this so it's not necessary to input the locale anymore. How do I get this upstream?" Alex Martelli said, "Oh, well you just email this mailing list, Python-Dev, and you can submit the patch."

> **Brett Cannon: 'Alex Martelli said, "Oh, well you just email this mailing list, Python-Dev, and you can submit the patch."'**

So, I emailed the list and I think Skip Montanaro was the first person to respond. Skip just said, "Yeah, that's great, just upload the file and we'll work at it and accept it." I thought that was awesome. I was able to contribute to this project and this language, which I thought was really interesting.

> **Brett Cannon: 'I was able to contribute to this project and this language, which I thought was really interesting.'**

All of this happened during a gap year I was taking between undergraduate and graduate school. I was trying to get into graduate school for computer science and I knew that I was going to need some more programming experience, beyond the courses I was taking. I thought that I could contribute to Python and help out. I had all the time in the world back then, so I decided I'd get involved.

> **Brett Cannon: 'I decided I'd get involved.'**

I got on the mailing list and I lurked around asking questions. Then in that same year, I offered to start taking up the Python-Dev summaries, which had stopped at that point. Once again, I figured I had the time to do it, and I realized it was a good way for me to learn, because it forced me to read every single solitary email in Python-Dev.

One interesting side effect was that I got to know about any small issues that nobody had time to take care of, so I saw anything that cropped up before almost anybody else. I was able to very easily pick up small issues to fix and learn, and I was able to continually do that.

In the guise of the Python-Dev summaries, I got to ask more and more questions.

At some point, I knew enough, and I became a core developer right after the first PyCon (at least the first conference labeled PyCon), in 2003. At that point I was hooked. I'd got to know the team and the people had become friends of mine. I just enjoyed it so much and it was fun, so I stuck with it and I've never really stopped for longer than a month since.

> **https://wiki.python.org/moin/GetInvolved**

That doesn't mean that you have to be a core developer to get into the Python community. As long you enjoy it, you can get hooked however it makes sense to you.

Driscoll: What then made you decide to start blogging and writing about Python?

Cannon: Blogging is one of those ways to get involved and since I enjoy writing, that medium happened to fit the way that I like to communicate. I started doing it way back when, and I've more or less consistently done it ever since. I always enjoy that aspect of dispensing knowledge to the world as best as I can.

Driscoll: Was it important that you got into Python at just the right time? Do you recommend getting in early on projects?

Cannon: Yes, it was one of those situations where I was in the right place at the right time, and with the free time I needed to get going. I managed to start when I had enough time to contribute as much as I wanted.

I also got started when the Python project wasn't that big. I remember when I started my master's degree, people would ask what I did in my spare time. When I said I contributed to Python, they'd reply, "Is that the language with the white space?" So I've just been doing this for a long time.

So yes, I got involved in the project at an ideal point, before interest in the language surged around 2005. I sometimes wish that I'd been able to get started with it earlier somehow, but I'd have been younger, so that might not have worked. So it was serendipitous that it all just came together when it did.

Driscoll: What parts of Python have you actively contributed to? Is there a module that you helped start or you had a major influence on, such as the `datetime` module?

Cannon: My influence was actually the `time` module. I predate the `datetime` module! The first modules that I ever authored were the `dummy_thread` and `dummy_threading` modules that were in Python 2.

That was another one of those instances where someone came forward and recommended it as a cool thing to do. They said they'd get to it, but over time they didn't get to it, so I emailed them saying, "Hey, are you going to get to this?" They said no, but that it would still be a useful thing to do, so I did it. Those were the first modules that I ever authored from scratch.

I've essentially touched, I think, everything in the Python language at this point. I've even touched the parser, which very few people ever have to touch. I think that I helped to write warnings for some tokenization thing at one point. I played a big part in the compiler, when we switched from going from a concrete syntax tree to byte code, to then having a proper concrete syntax tree, to an abstract syntax tree to Python.

> **Brett Cannon: 'I've essentially touched, I think, everything in the Python language at this point.'**

Jeremy Hilton had started that project, and Guido van Rossum basically gave everyone an ultimatum, because the project had been taking years to finish. So Guido said, "You have until the next release to finish this."

> **Brett Cannon: 'So Guido said, "You have until the next release to finish this."'**

I jumped in and helped Jeremy to carry it the last half of the way. I did a similar thing with the `warnings` module. Neil Norbits had started to implement it, but he kind of drifted off the project, so I picked it up and finished it the rest of the way. That's how I ended up being one of the people who knew the `warnings` module a little too well!

What else has led me to becoming so involved in Python? Probably the one thing that I'm most known for is `importlib`. I wrote most of the current implementation of `import` (all of it for Python 3.3) and then Nick Coghlan and Eric Snow helped a lot subsequently, but the whole `importlib` package was my doing. Those are the ones that come to mind in terms of what came directly from me, but I've basically just touched everything everywhere. I can't keep track anymore after 14 years!

Driscoll: I know what you mean. I hate it when I come across some code and I think, "Who wrote this, and why is it so bad?" I then remember that I wrote it a good two years ago!

Cannon: Yeah, if you manage to read your own code from six months ago and it still looks good, then there's probably something wrong. It usually means you haven't learned something new yet.

> **Brett Cannon: 'If you manage to read your own code from six months ago and it still looks good...it usually means you haven't learned something new yet.'**

Driscoll: What do you consider to be the best thing about being a core developer of Python?

Cannon: Probably just the friendships that I've made through being one. A lot of the core developers are friends of mine.

We get together once a year and I get to spend almost 24 hours a day for a whole week with a lot of these people. That's on top of the time I get to spend with them online throughout the rest of the year. It's probably more time than I get to spend with a lot of my friends, because how often do you actually get to take basically a full week of vacation with good friends of yours?

So yeah, it's honestly the friendships at this point. It's being able to hang out and work with these people, learn from them and enjoy what we do and keep doing that.

I don't think about the impact of Python very often. It's a little mind-boggling sometimes to think about, so I try not to dwell on it. I don't want any form of an ego because of it, so I try to actively not think about it too much. If I do just sit here and think about working on this language that's used by however many millions of developers, then that's a bit of an eye-opener. It's kind of cool to be able to say that I work on that, but primarily it's about getting to work with friends.

I still remember very clearly when I first joined the team, and even further back when I joined the mailing list, so although people say I'm one of these big high-up leads on the Python developer team, I've never fully acclimated to that idea. I just don't think of myself that way. Guido famously was once asked at Google, "On a scale of one to ten, how well do you know Python?" He said an eight.

> **'Guido famously was once asked at Google, "On a scale of one to ten, how well do you know Python?" He said an eight.'**

No one knows the entire system, because it's way too big a program to know. We can all fit the basic semantics in our heads, but not all the intricate details of how it actually works. How many people know descriptors or meta classes like the back of their hand? I have to look up that stuff on occasion, so nobody knows the whole system.

Driscoll: So where do you see Python going as a language, as a whole? Do you see it getting more popular in certain fields, or is Python getting into legacy status like C++?

Cannon: Python is in an interesting position today, where there are very few places where Python hasn't penetrated into as a major player. Sure, there are certain areas, like low-level operating systems and kernel development, that don't suit Python, but otherwise it can feel like Python is pretty much everywhere.

The one place I know we're still second with Python is in data science. I think our growth trends project that Python won't immediately overtake R as a data science language in the next couple of years at least. But long term, I do think that Python will catch up. Otherwise, I just don't know very many other fields, that don't require a systems language, where we aren't competitive for first place with Python.

I suppose another area, where Python isn't so strong, may be desktop apps, to a certain extent. Even on the desktop, people use us, so it's not like it's devoid, but there's just a lot of competition in that space. In the long term, and we might even be there already, we will hit the tipping point where there's so much Python code everywhere, that Python itself will probably never go away.

> **Brett Cannon: 'In the long term, and we might even be there already, we will hit the tipping point where there's so much Python code everywhere, that Python itself will probably never go away.'**

Hopefully, Python will never be uttered in the same passing breath as COBOL, and maybe we'll be loved a little bit more and for longer, but I don't see us ever really going anywhere. I think there's just too much code at this point to have us ever disappear.

Driscoll: Python is one of the major languages in the current AI and machine learning boom. What do you think makes Python such a good language for this?

Cannon: I think the ease of learning Python is what makes it good for AI. The people currently working in AI has expanded beyond just software developers, and now encompasses people like data scientists, who do not write code constantly.

That means that there is a desire for a programming language that can be easily taught to non-programmers. Python fits that need nicely. You can look at how Python has garnered traction with people in the sciences and in computer science education, to see how this is not a new trend.

Driscoll: Should people move over to Python 3 now?

Cannon: As someone who helped to make Python 3 come about, I'm not exactly an unbiased person to ask about this. I obviously think people should make the switch to Python 3 immediately, to gain the benefits of what has been added to the language since Python 3.0 first came out.

> **Brett Cannon: 'I hope people realize that the transition to Python 3 can be done gradually, so the switch doesn't have to be abrupt or especially painful.'**

I hope people realize that the transition to Python 3 can be done gradually, so the switch doesn't have to be abrupt or especially painful. Instagram switched in nine months, while continuing to develop new features, which shows that it can be done.

Driscoll: Looking ahead, what's happening with Python 4?

Cannon: The Python 4 thing is a whole conversation of its own, of course. I haven't heard much about Python 4, and I'd be happy to hear about it. It's mythical and it doesn't exist. Python 4 is like Py4k dreaming versus Py3k. Just where could the language go?

When it becomes time to do Python 4, we'll probably clean up the standard library a good amount and strip it down. There are some language elements we'll probably finally get rid of, instead of leaving them in there for compatibility with Python 2.

> **Brett Cannon: 'When it's time to do Python 4, we'll probably clean up the standard library a good amount, and strip it down.'**

For Python 4, we'll likely have a tracing garbage collector, instead of reference counting to get that parallelism. I don't know yet, but that's where I see it going: more or less the same, especially because we've come to rely more on the things that the community has built up around Python. I mean, one of the reasons we have huge standard libraries, is because it negates the internet, right?

Python itself predates Unicode as an official standard, because Python first went public in February 1991 and Unicode 1.0 went final in October 1991. I wasn't aware of that. I had to look it up, because it's one of those things where people ask me, "Hey, why didn't you do Unicode from the beginning like Java?" It's like, well, we predate Unicode, so that's why!

So in the future, I don't think the standard library will need to be quite as big as it is today. We don't need it to be if you can just `pip` install the equivalent libraries.

We're lucky enough to have a vibrant community, so we have lots of alternative third-party libraries that are of such a high standard, that we can probably thin out the standard library and lower the maintenance burden on the core developers. I think we can do this in some future Python releases without any risk to the community being able to access quality modules. I think it'll make Python easier and leaner, and just better to work with.

> **Brett Cannon: 'So in Python 4, I don't think the standard library will need to be quite as big as it is today.'**

That's what I suspect we'll do, but I don't get to make that call. It sounds like a good dream anyway. So yes, hopefully! I'm yet to have anyone tell me I'm completely insane when I answer questions about Python 4 with these ideas, which is a good litmus test.

Driscoll: What do you think is driving the recent and growing interest in MicroPython?

Cannon: People do keep asking me about writing about MicroPython. While I don't use it myself, I think that it must be getting bigger, because I keep getting asked about it! I'm willing to bet it's because of the education sector, with a lot of people using microbits and all that stuff. So that's probably where all the MicroPython interest is coming from.

Driscoll: How can we all start to contribute to the Python language? How do we get started?

Cannon: We have this thing called the Dev Guide, which I started writing back in 2011. Its full name is the *Python Developer's Guide*. Basically, the Dev Guide outlines everything you need to know so that you can contribute to the Python language.

> **Brett Cannon: 'The Dev Guide outlines everything you need to know so that you can contribute to the Python language.'**

The Dev Guide (*https://devguide.python.org/*) shows you how to get the Python source code, compile it and run the test suite. It offers suggestions for how you can find things that you'd like to contribute. You'll also find the documentation for core developers, which shows you how you can do a code review and everything else.

The Dev Guide is a rather large document at this point and it's kind of taken on a life of its own. I just tell people to go and read the Dev Guide, and try to have an idea about what you want to help with. Pick a module that you're really familiar with, that you could help to fix bugs in, or that you feel very comfortable with.

We have a core mentorship mailing list as well, which is not archived on purpose so that you can ask *any* question, and you don't have to worry about someone finding it five years later. So sign up for core mentorship, read the Dev Guide and then find something that you want to do!

Driscoll: Can we contribute to Python through code reviews?

Cannon: Yes, in fact at this point I've actually started to try to nudge people towards doing code reviews, so if you're really familiar with a module and there's a pull request on GitHub for it, please go for it and do a code review for that pull request.

If you feel comfortable doing code reviews and reviewing stuff on a module that you use regularly or not, that's a really great way to contribute to the development of the Python language.

> **Brett Cannon: 'If you feel comfortable doing code reviews and reviewing stuff on a module that you use regularly or not, that's a really great way to contribute to the development of the Python language.'**

The biggest limitation we have, in driving Python forwards, is the bandwidth on the core developers. So your code reviews can really help to make the projects easier to manage. Please help us to get more patches in, and bugs fixed, by joining in.

Driscoll: How else can we contribute to the Python language?

Cannon: A big help to the Python community is to answer questions that you see people asking about Python, and to answer those questions by just being open and honest. It's also important, of course, not to be a jerk when you talk about Python. It's fine to just be nice about it.

Driscoll: Are there any Python projects downstream that someone can jump in and contribute towards?

Cannon: Yes, if you don't find a current module that interests you, then you might find it interesting to contribute to some of the Python projects more downstream that need the help. For instance, the next version of the Python package index can always use some help. Jump on board if you find something downstream that you find interesting.

Driscoll: How about starter projects?

Cannon: Honestly, it's really kind of hard to have starter projects. We typically have enough people who are involved and watching to just jump on and fix them instantly. So it's hard to get started sometimes, which is why I'm starting to push for more of the pull request reviewing.

Driscoll: During PyCon, I see that there's usually a sprint set on the Python language. What sort of things do you guys do in those PyCon sprints?

Cannon: I've led a number of those PyCon sprints myself, and what we usually do is sit the Python core team down around some tables in one of the sprint rooms, and more or less just say, "Hey, if you want to contribute then come on in."

We tell PyCon sprint attendees the exact same things that we say to everyone who wants to contribute remotely: here's the Dev Guide, read it, get your tool chain up and running, and look for something to work on. If you find something then go for it.

> **Brett Cannon: 'We tell PyCon sprint attendees...here's the Dev Guide, read it, get your tool chain up and running, and look for something to work on.'**

Of course, at the sprints, we're there in the room to answer any questions that anyone may have. Typically, someone like R. David Murray will find a list of easy bugs to hand out to people in the sprint room. It's a great opportunity for people to come in and say hello. If they want to start contributing, then they have core Python people in the room, so they have a quick turnaround time for answers, instead of having to wait until someone sees the email and replies. It's very much just turn to the person to your left, or to your right, and you can ask and you get your answer.

Sometimes we'll give a short presentation to set out where we're going during the sprint, and if people can join in then that's great. We say, "Here are the tools, here's how you run the build, and here's how you run the tests." Then we get coding.

The sprints are very laid back and relaxing compared to the rest of a conference. I thoroughly recommend them when you can make them. It's just not as hectic in a sprint room as in the main area of a show. That's because there are less people, and everyone's just kind of sitting down and relaxing. There are no transitions, except to and from lunch, and it's easier to find people to have conversations with, which is great. So sprints are definitely fun to go to, and I'm going to try to go to one in the next year or two if I can.

> **Brett Cannon: 'We say, "Here are the tools, here's how you run the build, and here's how you run the tests." Then we get coding.'**

Driscoll: Some other teams have nice little enticements too, like if you are helping out with Russell Keith-Magee's BeeWare project, where you get a challenge coin on your first contribution. Have you seen those?

Cannon: Yes, if you help Russell's project out he gives you a challenge coin. It's a big and impressive metal coin. The one I'm holding in my hand right now is one that I earned from Russell and it takes up a good chunk of my Nexus 5X screen!

Here's how I earned my challenge coin from Russell: if you make a contribution that the BeeWare project accepts, such as docs or what have you, then you get one of these coins the next time you see Russell in person. So in my case, I happened to be on Twitter one day when Russell tweeted about an example repo, and I found a couple of typos. I sent a pull request to get them fixed and that's how I finally got my coin. I'd been wanting one for ages, because I think it is a really cool token of appreciation, and anyone can earn one if they contribute.

If you don't know anything about challenge coins, then 99% Invisible had a really good podcast episode explaining these things (`https://99percentinvisible.org/episode/coin-check/`).

> **Brett Cannon: 'If you don't know anything about challenge coins, then 99% Invisible had a really good podcast episode explaining these things.'**

Driscoll: Does the Python core team offer some incentives like Russell's challenge coins? What do you feel is the core spirit and incentive for people to contribute to the Python language?

Cannon: I've always wanted to make a challenge coin for Python, both for people who are core developers and for people who have contributed a patch. That's a neat idea. But I also don't travel as much as Russell, so it's a little harder because I'd need to be at the conferences that people are attending in order to give them the coins. But it's a cool idea and I wish more projects did it.

The Python core typically takes a very, kind of, passive approach to incentives. It's true, but that is really just because we're putting most of our time into the Python language elements that we want to get done, and we know that a lot of people are going to appreciate. That really is our deep incentive to contribute to Python, and I welcome everyone to join in, whether remotely, or during a conference sprint.

Driscoll: Thank you, Brett Cannon.

2

STEVE HOLDEN

Steve Holden is a British computer programmer and a former chairman and director of the Python Software Foundation (PSF). He is the author of *Python Web Programming* and co-authored the third edition of *Python in a Nutshell* with Alex Martelli and Anna Ravenscroft. Steve works as chief technical officer at Global Stress Index, a stress management start-up in the UK, where he oversees the application of technology producing systems. A career promoting the Python language has taken Steve around the world. He continues to support open source Python projects and speak at tech conferences.

Discussion themes: PyCon, the PSF, the future of Python.
Catch up with Steve Holden here: @holdenweb

Mike Driscoll: So could you tell me why you decided to become a computer programmer?

Steve Holden: In essence, I was very fond of electronics in my early teens. I switched from chemistry to electronics because a chemistry teacher turned me off the subject.

So I started my career at the age of 15 as a trainee production engineer in a television factory. After 18 months, that wasn't really going as well as it should. I began to look around for new employment and I saw a job advertising a junior technician role at the computing laboratory, at my local university in Bradford. So I applied for the job and when I got there, it turned out that junior technician was just a job grade. What they actually wanted was a keypunch operator.

The director of the lab thought that I was in danger of going off the rails. He decided that I should take a job with the laboratory for six months and learn about computers. So obviously I didn't get into the electronics side of it, because in those days, computer maintenance was an extremely specialized job. But I learned how to operate a computer and I learned how to program. That was the start of my career in computing.

Driscoll: That makes sense to me! So what made you start using Python and what makes it special to you?

Holden: Well, in the early 1970s, I developed an interest in object-oriented programming when I finally, at the age of 23, went to university. I came across some of the early papers on Smalltalk from Alan Kay's group at Xerox PARC.

> **Steve Holden: 'In the early 1970s I developed an interest in object-oriented programming.'**

The group seemed to have a very novel approach to computing, so I got interested in Smalltalk. Eventually, about 12 years later, when I was working at Manchester University, I actually got the chance to play with Smalltalk for the first time. I got a research student to implement it for me. There was no UK implementation of Smalltalk at the time. I discovered that actually I didn't really like Smalltalk very much. So I gave up on object-oriented programming for about another 10 years.

It was actually when I moved to the United States that I came across a book on Python. I think it was *Learning Python*, which was at that time by Mark Lutz and David Ascher. I realized that Python was the language for me! Python is a sensible, comprehensible, and understandable way to do object-oriented programming.

> **Steve Holden: 'I found that my knowledge of the language grew very quickly and pretty soon I was answering a lot of questions.'**

I did what people did in those days, which was to join the Python list. I found that my knowledge of the language grew very quickly and pretty soon I was answering a lot of questions. I think that in total I was active on comp.lang.python for about eight years. I made almost 200,000 posts! That's a lot of posts! Although unfortunately, I think that Google has let most of that stuff disappear now, so the history is gone from comp.lang.python.

Driscoll: Python is being used now in AI and machine learning. What do you think makes Python so popular?

Holden: Python has several advantages: it's easy to read and you can experiment interactively with objects that you create in a console or IDE. Python also provides relatively easy ways to interact with compiled languages that provide speed in large calculations (nobody expects the Spanish Inquisition).

Driscoll: Do you think that there are any problems currently with the Python language or its community?

Holden: The Python community (which is actually a large number of intersecting communities) just seems to go from strength to strength.

I am happy to say that Python appears to be widely accepted as a language, with a friendly and welcoming community. The Python Software Foundation (PSF) is now in a position to help to fund volunteer activities and offer a financial umbrella, as long as those activities promote and support the mission of the PSF.

> **Steve Holden: 'The Python Software Foundation (PSF) is now in a position to help to fund volunteer activities and offer a financial umbrella.'**

Having just completed writing the third edition of *Python in a Nutshell*, with Alex Martelli and Anna Ravenscroft, I would say that the language is in pretty good shape. However, I think that the new asynchronous primitives are proving to be more difficult for the average programmer to learn than they should be.

Guido van Rossum and the other core developers have done a great job of not distorting the language too far in order to make the additions. But the asynchronous paradigm, that is so familiar to Twisted developers, isn't quite as intuitively obvious as a simple synchronous task specification.

> **Steve Holden: 'I am a little concerned that Python development isn't doing a whole lot for the average mainstream user.'**

To be frank, I am a little concerned that Python development isn't doing a whole lot for the average mainstream user. A huge amount of work has been done to bring asynchronous programming into the language, which now includes a cooperative multitasking mechanism that obviates the need for threads.

As this work has proceeded, the developers have perceived a need for values that are private to the execution context of a specific asynchronous computation. You can think of them as `asyncio`'s equivalent of thread-local variables. As I've followed discussions on the Python-Dev list, I've seen much erudite discussion of issues that I suspect will never impact 99.5% of Python users. So I am thankful that Python is so dedicated to backward compatibility!

> **Steve Holden: 'I've seen much erudite discussion of issues that I suspect will never impact 99.5% of Python users.'**

I feel similarly, although rather less strongly, about the introduction of annotations to Python. They were first proposed as an entirely optional element of the language, but because people are using them, they are raising issues that are increasing the pressure to allow annotations in places like the standard library.

I'd like it to be possible for beginners to continue to learn the language, while remaining totally unaware of even the possibility of annotations, which can then be added later and completely orthogonally to the rest of the language. I'm not confident that this will continue to be the case.

Looking on the bright side, the relatively simple development of the f-string notation has been so enthusiastically adopted by the Python 3 community, that lots of code is being written that won't run on 3.5, simply because it uses f-strings. As usual, Dave Beazley has found diabolical things to do with f-strings, which is always fun.

Driscoll: How can we overcome those issues?

Holden: I'm not sure that there's any need for huge efforts to overcome those issues. It's important not to become complacent and to keep up the efforts to improve the language and broaden its community to become ever larger and more diverse. PyCon proved that technical communities can, to a large extent, be self-organizing.

Mike Driscoll: I know that you have been the chairman of PSF and PyCon in the past. How did you first become involved?

Holden: I went to my first, and effectively the last, International Python Conference in 2002. While the content was great, the event was run by a commercial group that did a lot of business with Guido's then employer, so it was geared to those who had the budget to attend.

While this had been fine in the early days of the language, it was obvious to me that if Python was going to be really popular, then its conference needed to offer a home to many more people. This included the people that I was engaging with on a daily basis on comp.lang.python.

> **Steve Holden: 'If Python was going to be really popular, then its conference needed to offer a home to many more people.'**

At the end of that conference, Guido made an announcement about the Python Software Authority (PSA), a more-or-less national governance body. PSA was to be replaced by a non-profit foundation. Guido also announced the creation of a mailing list to discuss conferences, which I eagerly anticipated!

Sadly, the archives (`https://mail.python.org/pipermail/conferences/`) only appear to go back to May 2009. But I remember when I last looked at the complete collection, my memory of waiting a long time for anything to appear was completely false. It took me about two days to become the first poster in the list. I expressed my opinion that the community could and would do a better job of organizing the conference, on a purely community basis.

> **Steve Holden: 'I expressed my opinion that the community could and would do a better job of organizing the conference.'**

I had the good fortune, completely by accident, to move to Virginia. This was within 20 or 30 miles of where Guido, Jeremy Hylton, Barry Warsaw, and Fred Drake were working at different places, while they collaborated on core Python.

That crew, along with Tim Peters, who had until then lived in Boston, got together as employees of a company called BeOS. It looked like that collaboration had a bright future and so it was a terrible blow when it became obvious after about six months that BeOS was in trouble. Fortunately, Zope Corporation, which is now Digital Creations, rented an office space for them and they established PythonLabs.

Driscoll: How did you start working with the Python team?

Holden: I had become known due to my voluminous contributions on comp.lang.python and the publication of Python Web Programming in 2002.

So when I contacted Guido and suggested that we meet for lunch, he invited me out to the office of PythonLabs. I met all five of the team and then we went out for a Chinese lunch at a place close by. These meetings became regular events every couple of weeks or so and one of the topics of discussion became whether the community really could get behind the idea of having no professional organizers.

> **Steve Holden: 'One of the topics of discussion became whether the community really could get behind the idea of having no professional organizers.'**

I think by the late 1990s, Guido realized that something a bit more formal was required and so the guys from PythonLabs started the PSF and acquired a certain amount of donated funding. I explained that I'd been the treasurer of DECUS UK & Ireland in the past and had experience of community conferences. Guido said that if I would agree to chair the conference, then the PSF would underwrite the costs.

We rented space in The George Washington University's Cafritz Conference Center and announced the dates, which received general excitement. Then the informal team quickly established the PyCon-organizers list. I remember that we got a lot of help from Nate Torkington, who had established the YAPC (Yet Another Perl Conference) idea.

> **Steve Holden: 'The ethos soon emerged that everything possible would be done by volunteers, to keep costs down.'**

The ethos soon emerged that everything possible would be done by volunteers, to keep costs down. Catherine Devlin stepped in to organize the food (taking account of everyone's dietary preferences is an impossible task). I can't even remember how the tickets were sold, since utility sites weren't available then.

About 250 people turned up for the conference, which was preceded by a two-day sprint and tutorials session. All talks were well attended. There was a real buzz and I went around trying to make sure that everyone got onto the internet.

That conference brought the Twisted team together in person for the first time. When I learned that they were having networking problems (most systems back in those days still needed an Ethernet cable), I impressed them by installing a local 100 MHz hub just for them.

Driscoll: Was the conference a financial success?

Holden: At the end of the conference, I announced that it appeared that the event had made roughly $17,000 for the PSF.

Guido proposed that I be given half of the profits, but I objected on the grounds that the PSF needed to build up its reserves. He also proposed me as a PSF member, an honour that I was happy to accept. I was duly voted in.

At OSCON that year, I interviewed Guido (`http://www.onlamp.com/pub/a/python/2003/08/14/gvr_interview.html`) and he talked about the need to get some more experienced hands involved with the PSF, which at the time he was leading due to the recognition that his name lent to the enterprise.

> **Steve Holden: 'I've never been a big fan of community events becoming the property of individuals.'**

At the end of the second PyCon, which was in the same venue a year later, I announced that I would chair one more conference. I've never been a big fan of community events becoming the property of individuals and chairing had been taking up an enormous amount of my time. Fortunately, most of my income back then came from teaching work and flexible consulting, that I could do largely from home.

If memory serves me correctly, it was that year that I was elected to the PSF board. Guido stood down as chairman and the board elected Stephan Deibel to replace him, asking Guido to continue to serve as titular present. This meant that what time he had available could be focused on development, rather than administrivia.

Driscoll: So, at what point did you step down from your role as chair of the conference?

Holden: At the end of the third PyCon, which was again and for the final time in Washington DC, nobody had stood up to chair the next conference. I couldn't even tell them that there was going to be a conference the following year, let alone when and where it would be.

> **Steve Holden: 'I held firm in my belief that if PyCon was going to make it, then even broader support needed to be attracted from the community.'**

I received several requests to chair one more conference, but I held firm in my belief that if PyCon was going to make it, then even broader support needed to be attracted from the community. About two months later, Andrew Kuchling approached me to ask what was involved and bless him he ran the next two conferences, which were held in Dallas, Texas. They marked the transition to using fully commercial venues and with that, PyCon has gone from strength to strength.

Driscoll: If someone wants to learn programming, why should they choose Python?

Holden: That depends on what age they are. I'd suggest that up to about the age of ten, a visual programming system like Scratch might be more appropriate.

Beyond that age, Python is definitely accessible enough to be a good first programming language. There is a huge amount of open source Python code in diverse areas. Nowadays, whatever field you work in, it's likely that there will be some Python code that you can use as a starting point.

> **Steve Holden: 'Python is definitely accessible enough to be a good first programming language.'**

Driscoll: So what coding techniques do you recommend?

Holden: I'm a big fan of test-driven development, despite having spent my first 30 years as a programmer not doing it. I see Agile as being more desirable from a business point of view, because it allows all stakeholders to select the work that's going to add most value to the business.

I've just spent almost a year and a half working with a perversion of that approach. I'm looking forward to validating in my new job that when run sensibly, Agile methods are a productive way to work. But I see Agile less as a coding technique and more as a development management methodology.

Pair programming isn't used as much as it used to be, but I think that from a technology transfer point of view, it's an incredible communications tool. Younger programmers don't seem to spend much time on career development, but as a manager I want to see my staff growing and learning. Pair programming is one way that they can acquire new skills relatively painlessly.

Driscoll: After learning the basics of Python, what next?

Holden: Look around for a problem that interests you and see if there are any open source projects in that area.

> **Steve Holden: 'While every new programmer likes to think that they can break ground, it's actually much easier to learn by collaborating.'**

While every new programmer likes to think that they can break ground, it's actually much easier to learn by collaborating in a team that knows what it's doing. Teamwork can teach you the practical software engineering skills that are so valuable in becoming an effective programmer.

People like to say that anyone can code, but signs are now emerging that this may not be true. Anyway, being able to code alone is nowhere near enough to build practical, functional and maintainable systems. Acquiring those other skills shouldn't be left until you have mastered programming.

Mike Driscoll: What about Python today most excites you?

Holden: The really exciting thing is the continued development of Python communities and the increase in Python usage, especially in education. This will ensure that relatively comprehensible programming tools will be readily available to anyone that needs them over the next 20 years.

I have on my desk a FiPy device that has Wi-Fi, Bluetooth, LoRa, Sigfox, and cellular communications on-chip, controlled by a MicroPython controller that, besides having the usual hardware bells and whistles, like digital inputs and outputs, gives REPL access to all of that functionality. I can hardly wait to retire and play with these things properly. Imagine what is going to become available over the next 10 years!

Driscoll: Where do you see the Python language going in the future?

Holden: I'm not really sure where the language is going. You hear loose talk of Python 4. To my mind though, Python is now at the stage where it's complex enough.

> **Steve Holden: 'You hear loose talk of Python 4. To my mind though, Python is now at the stage where it's complex enough.'**

Python hasn't bloated in the same way that I think the Java environment has. At that maturity level, I think it's rather more likely that Python's ideas will spawn other, perhaps more specialized, languages aimed at particular areas of application. I see this as fundamentally healthy and I have no wish to make all programmers use Python for everything; language choices should be made on pragmatic grounds.

I've never been much of a one for pushing for change. Enough smart people are thinking about that already. So mostly I lurk on Python-Dev and occasionally interject a view from the consumer side, when I think that things are becoming a little too esoteric.

Driscoll: Should people move over to Python 3?

Holden: Only when they need to. There will inevitably be systems written in 2.7 that won't get migrated. I hope that their operators will collectively form an industry-wide support group, to extend the lifetimes of those systems beyond the 2020 deadline for Python-Dev support. However, anyone starting out with Python should clearly learn Python 3 and that is increasingly the case.

Driscoll: Thank you, Steve Holden.

3

CAROL WILLING

Carol Willing is an American software developer and former director of the Python Software Foundation. For the last seven years, she has provided open source software and hardware development for Willing Consulting. Carol is a geek in residence at Fab Lab San Diego, a non-profit education center. She is a core developer for CPython and helps to organize both PyLadies San Diego and the San Diego Python User Group. Carol is also a research software engineer for Project Jupyter and an active contributor to open source Python projects. She is passionate about teaching tech as a speaker and writer.

Discussion themes: CPython, Jupyter, the PSF.
Catch up with Carol Willing here: @WillingCarol

Mike Driscoll: Could you give me a little background information about yourself?

Carol Willing: I am someone who got involved in computing in elementary school back in the 70s. I actually grew up in the shadow of Bell Labs. In a similar way to the Python community, they had outreach for young coders.

Then I had the opportunity in middle school to continue programming on the first TRS-80 and an Apple II. I always liked programming because it was about exploring something new. There was no internet then, so you pretty much just had the source code and some slim bit of documentation. You were the explorer of the computer, if you will. So it was really fun.

After that I got a degree in electrical engineering. While I was in college, I had the opportunity to run the cable television station on campus. I got to learn the technical side, as well as how to motivate people who were volunteers.

I really didn't work as an engineer until about six years into my career. I took a long break from work, but the whole time I was doing things like building a Linux network in my house. I decided that I really wanted to go back and do the development side, because that was what really rocked my world. I had an opportunity to work on the Jupyter team and that's what I'm doing now.

Driscoll: How did you go from being an electrical engineer back to programming? I know a lot of electrical engineers are more hardware oriented.

Willing: Well, I still have a real love for hardware and things like MicroPython and CircuitPython. That still interests me quite a bit, but I like the puzzle of programming.

> **Carol Willing: 'I like the puzzle of programming.'**

I think my first love was math and actually programming. The electrical engineering stuff that I liked to do was the digital communications theory. So it was really more math and software development than it was actually the hardware stuff.

Driscoll: How did you end up using Python, instead of Ruby or some other language?

Willing: Well, I had done C++, Java, and Ruby in the early Rails days. Then when I was looking seriously at computer languages, I realized that I was actually looking for a tech community that I would enjoy being in.

In Southern California, we have a lot of opportunities for meetups. For a while I dabbled in the Linux community. Then I actually started working with some people from OpenHatch on teaching people how to get involved in open source.

The more that I played around with Python, the more I started really enjoying the readability of it. Python made it easy to get things done and there were vast libraries out there. So that was my route to Python. It was a nonlinear path to the world of Python, but a good path.

Driscoll: Could you explain how you became a core developer of Python?

Willing: Yes, I got involved with organizing some of the talks and tutorials for PyCon several years ago. I attended, and it was surprising to me how many developers there were at the CPython sprints, but how few were women.

> **Carol Willing: 'It was surprising to me how many developers there were at the CPython sprints, but how few were women.'**

Nick Coghlan, and a couple of other people, were explaining to me how things worked. I felt that we needed better outreach, so I did a lot of work with the Python Developer's Guide and also outreach within the PyLadies community. I worked with Nick and Guido van Rossum on how we could better document what we were doing and make it more accessible. So that was the way that I became a core developer.

Jupyter relies really heavily on Python 3. So I think there's a strong need for voices from outside of the web community to also give back to the core language. I think that Python is a great language and there's so much opportunity. Even though Python has been around for 20 years, I think we've barely scratched the surface of where this language can take us.

> **Carol Willing: 'Even though Python has been around for 20 years, I think we've barely scratched the surface of where this language can take us.'**

Driscoll: So what parts of the library are you in charge of? What do you do as a core developer?

Willing: Right now, I'm mostly working on documentation and development tools guides. I also mentor some people in the community that are getting started developing with Python, or Core Python.

I get involved with things that we rely heavily on in Jupyter, like asynchronous stuff. If I had more time then I would be more involved on the CPython side. Right now, though, Jupyter has been growing in leaps and bounds, so it has kept us a little busy.

I also really love getting involved with education. I think that if you can make a language accessible to people, then you get lots of great ideas. That's part of the power of all the libraries that are out there in Python.

Driscoll: So what are you doing at the moment with the Python Software Foundation (PSF)?

Willing: I have just served two years as a director of the PSF. Right now, I'm involved with several of the working groups, such as marketing and science.

Really this year I'm focusing more on going out across the world to speak and share. I want to talk about the state of education surrounding Python, where we are with Python in general across many different disciplines, and also how that fits in with Jupyter. Then I'll also be involved again with PyCon and the tutorials. It's actually fun to read all of the proposals that people send in.

I'm relatively new to the marketing work group, but we're trying to explore other ways to engage the community globally, as well as sponsors. We want to highlight how Python is actually being used out in the real world. The marketing group is trying to come up with a stronger Twitter campaign, so that people have more of an idea about what the PSF does.

Mike Driscoll: What are the current goals for the PSF?

Willing: The mission of the PSF is to sustain the Python language itself and protect the copyrights. There is also a goal to grow the language and the use of the language globally in places that maybe aren't using Python already.

On a year-to-year basis, the goals may look a little bit different. Obviously, running PyCon is very important and will always be a goal of the PSF. Other things may be more strategic, such as deciding how we balance the requests for grants that come in, with other projects that we are funding.

Another thing that's really important across all of the open source world is the sustainability of projects and how you fund the infrastructure that these projects are running on. We've been very fortunate in the PSF to have had some wonderful donors within the community and sponsors. But if for some reason a sponsor went away, people would still expect PyPI to be up and running and also the website.

You need to build a long-term sustainability plan, so that you don't burn out your volunteers. The PSF also needs to provide the level of service that people have come to expect. I know Donald Stufft has done a few interviews on how much traffic PyPI routes a day. The figure is pretty phenomenal. PyPI is something that we all depend on. The PSF maintains the presence of Python within the world and the infrastructure that you may take for granted on a day-to-day basis as a developer.

> **Carol Willing: 'The PSF maintains the presence of Python within the world and the infrastructure that you may take for granted on a day-to-day basis as a developer.'**

Driscoll: So, I don't know if you can talk about this or not, but what do you do at Project Jupyter?

Willing: I can tell you what we do at Project Jupyter, because Jupyter is an open source project. It is funded with a scientific research project grants, as well as some corporate donations.

There are basically three major areas within Jupyter. There's the classic Jupyter Notebook, which grew out of the IPython Notebook. There are also the many different widgets and tools that integrate with the Notebook. Lastly there's JupyterHub, which is what I work specifically on.

JupyterHub looks at how you provide Notebooks to a group of people in a cluster. That could be in a small workshop, or a research lab. We're seeing a lot of use of JupyterHub within large academic institutions. Also, a lot of the researchers in high-performance computing are using JupyterHub for very numerically intensive processing.

> **Carol Willing: 'Basically JupyterLab will give you a streamlined IDE feel, with some nice functionality.'**

The next generation of the Notebook is JupyterLab. Basically, JupyterLab will give you a streamlined IDE feel, with some nice functionality. You can pull graphs out of the page and have them still sync and reflect what changes are happening.

JupyterLab is built to be extensible, so you can add things and customize them. I've been using JupyterLab probably for about a year and in different iterations. The feedback has been very positive and JupyterLab was shared at SciPy a year ago.

Driscoll: Do you need a subscription to use JupyterHub? How does that work?

Willing: No, JupyterHub is also a free open source project. So, if you had a bare-metal server, you could deploy it on your own server. You could just deploy JupyterHub on AWS, Azure, Google Cloud, or others like Rackspace.

We recently put together a guide to help people to set up a JupyterHub deployment using Kubernetes. That is actually working out really nicely. There are multiple methods for the authentication of users, because there's a lot of variability in how different academic institutions authenticate people.

> **Carol Willing: 'You can provide every student with a web account and they will have all of the same tools and the same experience.'**

You want something that we call a spawner, which will spawn an individual Jupyter Notebook instance for a person. That's why JupyterHub is attractive to universities. You can provide every student with a web account and they will have all of the same tools and the same experience. You don't have to deal with installation nightmares.

Driscoll: Do you work on IPython as well?

Willing: IPython is part of that whole Jupyter project, but the work that I do on IPython itself is minimal. I will occasionally help them to try out new releases.

Jupyter is all one big academic research project. We don't have an overabundance of marketing resources, but we're trying to spread the word. One of the things that I think is really powerful about Jupyter is that you can share information in such a way that people can interact with it easily. I've certainly seen students really gravitate towards Jupyter.

Driscoll: So what do you like about the Python community?

Willing: I think Brett Cannon and other people have said before that you come for the programming language, but you stay for the Python community. That really resonates. In the tech world, I don't know of any community that's been more welcoming than the Python community.

Carol Willing: 'You come for the programming language, but you stay for the Python community.'

So many thoughtful and talented people are willing to share their knowledge and ideas. I think that a lot of that comes from Guido himself and his willingness to have a language that's easy to use and easy to read. Guido also encourages people and answers questions because he wants a healthy Python community, as well as a healthy language. I think that is really important.

> **Carol Willing: 'Guido also encourages people and answers questions because he wants a healthy Python community, as well as a healthy language.'**

I think it's fun to see all of the different things that people are doing. As much as I love PyCon, I really love the regional conferences. That's where you really see the new stuff that is happening. You get different people's perspectives and find out what they are using Python for.

There's nothing like trying to teach new users how to do something, to make you realize that Python needs to improve the user experience somewhere. As a developer, it's not pleasant for me, so for a new learner, who doesn't necessarily know if their thing is configured correctly, it's even more unpleasant.

Driscoll: What is exciting you about Python at the moment?

Willing: I think you've gathered from our conversation so far that my interests are not related to just one thing.

One of the nice things about Python is that I can use the language if I'm doing embedded stuff, web stuff, scientific development, or analysis. I can certainly use Python for teaching kids or adults. There aren't a whole lot of languages that I can say are really strong across the board on all of those things. I think that Python really excels there.

> **Carol Willing: 'Learning and education are what excite me about Python. Python 3 is a pleasure to use for teaching.'**

Learning and education are what excite me about Python. Python 3 is a pleasure to use for teaching and f-strings have greatly simplified string formatting. MicroPython, CircuitPython, Raspberry Pi, micro:bit, and Jupyter have inspired more young people to make some really interesting projects. It was great fun to see the young developers at PyCon UK far exceed our expectations with their projects and lightning talks.

Driscoll: So, as a core developer of Python, where do you see the language going in the future?

Willing: I think we're going to continue to see growth in the scientific programming part of Python. So things that support the performance of Python as a language and async stability are going to continue to evolve. Beyond that, I think that Python is a pretty powerful and solid language. Even if you stopped development today, Python is a darn good language.

I think that the needs of the Python community are going to feed back into Python and influence where the language goes. It's great that we have more representation from different groups within the core development team. Smarter minds than mine could provide a better answer to your question. I'm sure that Guido has some things in mind for where he wants to see Python go.

> **Carol Willing: 'A better story in mobile is definitely needed. But you know, if there's a need then Python will get there.'**

Mobile development has been an Achilles' heel for Python for a long time. I'm hoping that some of the BeeWare stuff is going to help with the cross-compilation. A better story in mobile is definitely needed. But you know, if there's a need then Python will get there.

I think that the language is going to continue to move towards the stuff that's in Python 3. Some big code bases, like Instagram, have now transitioned from Python 2 to 3. While there is much Python 2.7 code still in production, great strides have been made by Instagram, as they shared in their PyCon 2017 keynote.

> **Carol Willing: 'It will vary by company, but at some point, business needs, such as security and maintainability, will start driving greater migration to Python 3.'**

There's more tooling around Python 3 and more testing tools, so it's less risky for companies to move some of their legacy code to Python 3, where it makes business sense to. It will vary by company, but at some point, business needs, such as security and maintainability, will start driving greater migration to Python 3. If you're starting a new project, then Python 3 is the best choice. New projects, especially when looking at microservices and AI, will further drive people to Python 3.

Driscoll: Why do you think that Python is being used so much for AI and machine learning?

Willing: The long history of Python being used in science and data science makes Python an excellent choice for AI. The rich ecosystem of Python libraries, including scikit-learn, NumPy, pandas, and Jupyter, gives researchers and creators a solid foundation for getting work done.

> **Carol Willing: 'The long history of Python being used in science and data science makes Python an excellent choice for AI.'**

Driscoll: How could Python be a better language for AI?

Willing: Sustaining the existing Python infrastructure and key libraries is critical for the fundamental growth of Python. A healthy and inclusive ecosystem, and corporate funding for sustainability, will help to continue the rapid growth of AI, deep learning, and machine learning.

Driscoll: Are there any changes that you hope to see in future Python releases?

Willing: I would love to see more task-oriented documentation to support the concurrency, async, parallelism, and distributed processing. We have had some wonderful enhancements in the past few releases, and it would be fantastic to help others to more easily use these enhancements.

Driscoll: Thank you, Carol Willing.

4

Glyph Lefkowitz

Glyph Lefkowitz is an American software engineer who has worked on numerous open source projects. Previous roles include senior software engineer at Apple, and today he works at Pilot.com, a bookkeeping service for start-ups. Glyph is the original founder of Twisted, a network programming framework written in Python. He continues to maintain Twisted and play an active role in the Twisted community. In 2009, Glyph was made a fellow of the Python Software Foundation (PSF). The PSF awarded Glyph its Community Service Award for contributions to the Python language in 2017.

Discussion themes: v2.7/v3.x, Python's future, diversity.
Catch up with Glyph Lefkowitz here: @glyph

Mike Driscoll: So how did you end up becoming a programmer?

Glyph Lefkowitz: Well, my programming path was somewhat circuitous. I started off programming as a kid, but I do not have the stereotypical story of learning BASIC, then Perl. There wasn't a linear progression, or some professional aspiration that I had to do programming.

I just wanted to make games like Zork when I was a kid. My dad is a professional programmer, so he tried to teach me APL. I did not take to programming quickly. I learned how to assign variables and that was it. I had no idea what variable assignment meant. That was where I stayed for about five years.

Then I learned HyperCard and I started to get the notion of control flow and loops. I tried to make video games with it. The whole time, for my entire childhood, I was trying to avoid learning to program. I was always looking for non-programmer stuff to do, because I was terrible at math.

> **Glyph Lefkowitz: 'The whole time, for my entire childhood, I was trying to avoid learning to program.'**

So after a while, HyperCard sort of got limiting. I got SuperCard and at some point, I learned what a variable was and how to make programs that would actually operate on data structures. Then I learned C++. Once I understood the power inherent in programming, after years of trying to avoid it, then I really got into it.

> **Glyph Lefkowitz: 'Once I understood the power inherent in programming, after years of trying to avoid it, then I really got into it.'**

I learned Java, I learned Perl, I learned Lisp and I learned Scheme, all in high school. I taught a programming class at my high school, so I got really into it by the time I was about 17. But it was quite a slog on the way up there.

Driscoll: So how did that end up pushing you from all those other languages into Python?

Lefkowitz: Well, by the time I started my professional career, I'd sort of settled on Java.

I had some really terrible experiences with the proprietary runtime, particularly for macOS, that shipped with Java. So I had professional experience with the runtimes being really bad. Basically, there was a bug in the windowing system that the application I was working on kind of leaned on.

The application could not be rearchitected to avoid tickling this bug, because the bug was connected with leaking large amounts of memory. So effectively the project that I was on died and I lost the job. I ended up being unemployed for a couple of months and as a result of that experience I thought well, screw Java, I'm not doing that anymore, mainly because of the runtime issues.

> **Glyph Lefkowitz: 'I ended up being unemployed for a couple of months and as a result of that experience I thought well, screw Java.'**

My very first reaction was to see what GNU had on offer for a Java compiler. I thought maybe I could do Java, but not touch the runtime stuff, because it was just too buggy. The conclusion from that was rapidly that none of that stuff worked.

So at the same time, my hobby project, which does exist to this day, was this online text-based game which I had written in Java. A tremendous amount of the work that I had done in Java was building up these hash tables full of objects with run methods.

There were then arguments to the run methods, which I would inject into them with reflection. The whole idea was that you were supposed to wire the game together at runtime. It was kind of user-programmable, but in a more restricted way.

Driscoll: So how did this game work?

Lefkowitz: You would have a set of building blocks that were somewhat constrained, so that if you made something, it could have game consequences and not just flavor text that it would print. So almost all of the code in the Java version was this tremendous amount of ceremony, associated with dynamically composing objects, out of other objects that might be arbitrary collections.

I reimplemented the whole thing in Python and I realized that you didn't need to do any of that stuff. Objects in Python were just these dynamic collections of things, that you could arbitrarily add attributes to and retrieve attributes from. You could look into other dicts and all that stuff.

> **Glyph Lefkowitz: 'I reimplemented the entire thing, which was about 25,000 lines of Java in 800 lines of Python, and I thought it was a much better program.'**

So I reimplemented the entire thing, which was about 25,000 lines of Java in 800 lines of Python, and I thought it was a much better program. Now granted, what I had implemented in Java was a crummy version of the Python object model, so it was particularly easy to implement.

One of my interests that has endured over many years is composability and the ability to automatically assemble. I want the ability to make programs self-symmetric, so that you can have a large number of implementations of the similar interface and compose them automatically. Python's metaprogramming facilities were in this wonderful sweet spot between say Lisp or Scheme, where there was so much power that nothing was compatible. No two people would write the same object model in those languages.

At the other end, with something like Java, everything was very standardized, but it didn't matter, because everything was also really tedious. You couldn't automatically pull things together and everything was very verbose, so it wasn't worth trying to do any metaprogramming.

Python is standard enough that things work together, but flexible and high-level enough that you get almost as much power as Lisp macros. So that's why I've stuck with it ever since, although because I know a bunch of other languages, I periodically venture into them. But Python is definitely my main language that I've built my career on.

> **Glyph Lefkowitz: 'Python is definitely my main language that I've built my career on.'**

Driscoll: Are you actually a core Python developer? I wasn't able to discover that information.

Lefkowitz: I'm not. I have attended a bunch of core Python developer events, because Twisted is a pretty high-profile Python project.

I went to a language summit a couple of years ago and I have triage permissions on the bug tracker. I'm on the Python security response team to provide a library perspective on this stuff. I also worked with Guido van Rossum a fair amount on asyncio getting integrated into the standard library. For instance, providing feedback on that and the experiences I've had with Twisted.

So I'm peripheral to Python core development, but not a member of the core team. I never really had the desire to get involved. I basically already spend way more time than I probably should doing volunteer open source development, to be adding to that by doing Python core stuff. A lot of people use Python professionally and want to give back, but I already give back.

Driscoll: So, now we're talking about Twisted, could you tell me about how Twisted came about and what inspired you to write it?

Lefkowitz: Well, it came about originally because of that very same video game that I was telling you about before. I started off in Python rewriting the Java version of the server that I had been working on.

The concurrency of that server was very heavily based on threads, because there were multiple players walking around and multiple autonomous agents doing various things. So there was just a big mess of threads in Java. There was no other way to do it and the whole ecosystem was kind of oriented around using lots of threads.

> **Glyph Lefkowitz: 'There was a time... when the term massively multithreaded was like a boast that projects would make.'**

In fact, I'll never forget this, there was a time, in the late 1990s and very early 2000s, when *massively multithreaded* was like a boast that projects would make. This was something positive that they were claiming about their project.

We had a similar type of architecture and it was a giant mess. There were tons and tons of horrible bugs that were the result of the incorrect management of threads. I don't remember exactly how I discovered it, but basically originally there were three threads for every connection: the reader thread, the writer thread and the logic thread.

My friend James Knight rewrote the client/server protocol for this game. I believe that when he rewrote it, he condensed down those three threads into a single thread per player, by using the select module.

Driscoll: What did this development mean for you?

Lefkowitz: I looked at the client/server protocol and I realized that there were multiple things I wanted to know about, that I might be able to do with a socket.

> **Glyph Lefkowitz: 'Once I found out about the select module, I read about it and it completely changed my conception of how programs worked.'**

So once I found out about the `select` module, I read about it and it completely changed my conception of how programs worked. As I mentioned before, my early introduction to programming was HyperCard, so I had this intuitive notion that the computer is idle and waiting for something to happen.

Driscoll: Where did you go from there?

Lefkowitz: So, after messing around with the `select` module for a day or two, I realized that you could have something that was on data received, or on connection started, and do something.

That was much more natural to me, because I had been using threads to sort of emulate this, but never felt really comfortable. At that time, I didn't have a good intuition about what happened when we started up a program. It started threads in the background, or something concurrent was happening, but I didn't really understand how the parallelism worked.

With `select`, you could see the parallelism because multiple connections would come in. Then there would just be multiple objects that I had instantiated and that had methods on them, which I was calling from this event loop. So building that up from the bottom gave me a much better understanding of how concurrency worked.

From there, the idea was that the game would be what these days you call an alternate reality game. It would be reaching out via various protocols to send you emails or send you text messages. This really dates the whole thing, because the web server was not the first thing I did and it was not really clear that the web thing was going to catch on.

> **Glyph Lefkowitz: 'The web was just a really slow and buggy native client that crashed a lot.'**

For us, the Twisted development team, the web was just a really slow and buggy native client that crashed a lot. We could write native clients in Python that would do exactly what we wanted. Security, of course, was not nearly the concern that it is today, so it wasn't as clear that we needed sandboxing. To be fair, browser security was also terrible at the time, but it was not like we were really thinking about that. So that's how the project got built up into the multi-protocol Hydra that it is.

One of the reasons that Twisted existed in the form where it had this big standard library built in, was that we really wanted developers to rewrite their protocols in such a way that you did not need threads to speak to them. I still feel this way to a large extent today.

Driscoll: What lessons did you learn from the first Twisted releases?

Lefkowitz: Well, one lesson was that each time you made an object persistent, you were basically making a vow to support it for the rest of your natural life.

> **Glyph Lefkowitz: 'One lesson was that each time you made an object persistent, you were basically making a vow to support it for the rest of your natural life.'**

So we had all of these really crummy little classes that were dumb implementation details. They were exactly the kind of thing you would imagine if you got a bunch of bored 19-year-olds to write a bunch of production-critical server infrastructure. That's what we were doing and we ended up creating this very odd situation where we had these server files which were like dozens of dead objects from previous versions of the software.

We didn't know the files were in there because `pickle` has no way to visualize your object graph, or show you what's going on. So the main web server for Twistedmatrix.com, up until around 2009, was this 45 MB `pickle` file. We didn't know why it was so big, but that was how you would run it. You would just fire up a Python interpreter to run the reactor. We were living five to ten years in the future, but that wasn't necessarily always a good thing.

Driscoll: What problems did you run into?

Lefkowitz: We were sometimes trying to do things that were really bad decisions, because there was no tooling associated with them.

There was no supporting ecosystem, so we assumed that we could do something alternative that was not keeping all of our config and plain text files. We thought we could then somehow handwave all the benefits of version control and text diffing, and all the log processing tools would somehow arrive in our ecosystem, but they never did. So we've been trying to do less weird for the sake of weird in the last five to ten years of the project, which is still less than half its lifetime.

> **Glyph Lefkowitz: 'We've been trying to do less weird for the sake of weird in the last five to ten years of the project.'**

Driscoll: So you mentioned that you were helping with the `asyncio` and other library changes related to that. How do you see those changes affecting Twisted?

Lefkowitz: I actually wrote an article on my blog about this a while back. At the time, a vocal minority of Python users, who really didn't like Twisted to begin with, sort of rejoiced that the library changes would finally kill Twisted, because there would be no reason to use it anymore.

> **Glyph Lefkowitz: 'A vocal minority of Python users, who really didn't like Twisted to begin with, sort of rejoiced that the library changes would finally kill Twisted.'**

What I predicted at the time, and I think this prediction has largely borne out, was that sanctioning event-driven concurrency in the standard library, and saying this is the way that Python does concurrency, would prompt a lot of new interest in Twisted.

The whole Python stack has really been converging on this idea of event-driven concurrency being the right way to do things. Previously, Twisted had to be a good server framework that you could use to deploy your applications. It also had to be a good GUI client framework, that you could use to write direct line apps and desktop apps.

Twisted needed to be a solid implementation of a bunch of design patterns, but it also had to be its own little standard library. It had to paper over a bunch of issues in the Python standard library that had a really slow release cycle and you couldn't necessarily depend on for the applications.

> **Glyph Lefkowitz: 'This tool appeared to be proselytizing to them before it was solving their problems.'**

The sort of breaking point that Twisted reached, was that it also had to be this messenger for event-driven networking. People would come to Twisted wanting some feature, and then you would first have to sell them on the idea that async was a good idea at all. What this resulted in was that people would show up to Twisted with no shared expectations and no background. This tool appeared to be proselytizing to them before it was solving their problems.

In order to live in the Twisted ecosystem to some extent, to get the real benefits of it, you would have to start converting your code over to this async model, and that was a bunch of work. If you didn't know how it worked and it wasn't intuitive to you, it would be baffling. You would not be in a frame of mind where you'd be interested in hearing about it.

So the interesting thing is that even people who are stuck on Python 2.7, and will be for the next decade, show up to Twisted nowadays.

Driscoll: Why are people stuck on Python 2.7?

Lefkowitz: People kind of know that the standard library, like Python, has moved on. It's all event-driven now, it's all async, and they can't use `asyncio` because they're in a large corporate code base.

Initially the transition from Python 2 to Python 3 was, frankly, mismanaged. The core team, despite warnings from concerned users like myself, just didn't comprehend the scale of their own creation. They underestimated the migration effort by several orders of magnitude.

> **Glyph Lefkowitz: 'Initially the transition from Python 2 to Python 3 was, frankly, mismanaged.'**

The long life of Python 2 is a consequence of their responsible management of that mistake. The Python development team saw that users were not upgrading, and worked hard to understand why and to address the issues of big Python users. So it's not ideal, but it's significantly better than the alternative, which was for Python 3 to become Perl 6.

Driscoll: What's your opinion of Python 3?

Lefkowitz: I'm in Python 3 in my day job now and I love it. After much blood, sweat and tears, I think it actually is a better programming language than Python 2 was. I think that it resolves a lot of inconsistencies.

Most improvements should mirror quality of life issues and the really interesting stuff going on in Python is all in the ecosystem. I absolutely cannot wait for a PyPy 3.5, because one of the real downsides of using Python 3 at work is that I now have to deal with the fact that all of my code is 20 times slower.

When I do stuff for the Twisted ecosystem, and I run stuff on Twisted's infrastructure, we use Python 2.7 as a language everywhere, but we use PyPy as the runtime. It is just unbelievably fast! If you're running services, then they can run with a tenth of the resources.

A PyPy process will take 80 MB of memory, but once you're running that it will actually take more memory per interpreter, but less memory per object. So if you're doing any Python stuff at scale, I think PyPy is super interesting.

One of my continued bits of confusion about the Python community is that there's this thing out there which, for Python 2 anyway, just makes all of your code 20 times faster. This wasn't really super popular, in fact PyPy download stats still show that it's not as popular as Python 3, and Python 3 is really experiencing a huge uptick in popularity.

> **Glyph Lefkowitz: 'The lack of viable Python 3 implementation for PyPy is starting to hurt it quite a bit.'**

I do think that given that the uptake in popularity has happened, the lack of a viable Python 3 implementation for PyPy is starting to hurt it quite a bit. But it was around and very fast for a long time before Python 3 had even hit 10% of PyPy's downloads. So I keep wanting to predict that this is the year of PyPy on the desktop, but it just never seems to happen.

Driscoll: Why do you think PyPy has not taken off on the server?

Lefkowitz: I'm still not quite sure why, because especially for companies with significant infrastructure spend, it could save them literally millions of dollars a year to run.

You can tell companies that they will save millions of dollars a year if they rewrite all of their code. The problem is they would be taking a huge security risk, blowing up the size of their development team and making no feature progress in two years. That's a bad trade-off and I can see why you wouldn't want to do that.

With PyPy we say, "Why is that not the future? We just dropped in this new interpreter." There are reasons that we can't use it, such as that the scientific Python community's tooling does not work on PyPy yet. But that's actually the exception rather than the rule, and even NumPy programs largely work on PyPy. I wrote some OpenGL stuff last year that uses PyPy extensively and doing that was really interesting.

Driscoll: What do you like about PyPy?

Lefkowitz: You write an OpenGL program using CPython and it's struggling to stay at 50 frames per second. You do the same thing in PyPy and it's 300, 400 or 500 frames per second, not breaking a sweat and not taking up CPU.

> **Glyph Lefkowitz: 'Where I would like to see Python go is for it to adopt more advanced technology.'**

Where I would like to see Python go is for it to adopt more advanced technology, but for some reason we've collectively lagged behind. Another thing that I think will be critical for determining where Python goes is to what extent we can get away from *pip* as a tool for users to install applications.

I think that we need a better story for how you write cross-platform GUI code, even if it's really basic. For instance, `tkinter` is bad enough that people just don't use it. We need a better story for how you package applications.

I want to make an app that I can upload to the App Store, even before we start talking about mobile. There are all the issues of resource constraints that come along with that. I want to compile my app and put it on someone else's computer, but it is way too hard to do that right now.

Driscoll: Do you see making apps becoming easier?

Lefkowitz: I'm encouraged by projects like pybee/briefcase, and I think that they're starting to finally gain some traction.

They're a very small project with very big problems in front of them. But they're also very determined and committed, with real experience of navigating those issues. This is evidenced by Pythonista, the iOS Python app, which uses their code.

I think that the story around building and integrating Python programs is getting better all the time. I am optimistic that within the next five years, it won't be unusual to see apps that are fully written in Python, rather than the small handful of examples that we have now.

It would be a shame if the only way you could realistically get Python code from one computer to another was Docker. Python should be on your Mac, it should be on your Android, it should be on your Linux box, it should be in the cloud and it should be on your Raspberry Pi. In particular, with the emergence of the Internet of Things, I really wish more of those things were running Python web servers.

> **Glyph Lefkowitz: 'The mission is Python on every port, and we really feel like that's an important mission.'**

The mission is Python on every port, and we really feel like that's an important mission. So many services, the things that people actually use to talk to edge network devices such as Nginx, Apache, XM and BIND, are also in C.

We're writing all of our application code in these high-level languages. The things that are actually pulling the bytes off the wire and handing them to your application, then parsing them, are all barely-maintained C programs from 20 years ago. This is a real danger.

So the idea is that you can't do crypto in Python. Crypto primitives need to be in C, but those are a tiny part of a security application. Higher-level cryptographic constructions can (and really should) absolutely be assembled in Python, where you're dealing with composing multiple cryptographic primitives into a workable whole. Doing that composition in C is dangerous and error-prone.

In many cases, you have to drop down to a sublayer, but you have to write crypto primitives in a language where you can tell the underlying hardware to take fixed lengths of time to do things. So it has to be completely data input independent. It also has to be extremely fast, because you don't want to be paying a huge overhead to encrypt things. You just need to encrypt them no matter what.

Driscoll: Do you think that the Python language is here to stay?

Lefkowitz: Wow, that's an interesting question! I think that many languages that have had the lifetime that Python has had, have sort of slowly faded into legacy status.

Overall, I think one of the places that the Python language is going is forwards. It's still an unbelievably vibrant community and it's still growing. It was growing slowly at the beginning and it's growing slowly now, but it has been consistently growing over years and years. I think this is interesting because there are a lot of languages that have been gigantic flashes in the pan. Ruby was hugely popular for a while and then its popularity really plummeted with Rails losing popularity.

> **Glyph Lefkowitz: 'I think Python is going to have a much longer life than previous generations of languages.'**

I think Python is going to have a much longer life than previous generations of languages, which were in their heyday super-hot technology, and then faded away with the next generation of stuff. I think Python is becoming its own next generation. Ironically, I think that Python 3 is a very small part of that.

One thing that I really hope happens, and I think it's another one that hasn't yet, is Python in the browser. Skulpt, Pyjs, PyPy.js, and a bunch of other projects have kind of got things that are good proofs of concept, but again nobody's sitting down and going: "I'm a new Python programmer and I want to do a frontend Python app. What do I do?"

The answer to that is inevitably that the thing that actually lets you do what you want to do is only on Git master in this one project. You've got to check it out and check out another project. When you ask the question: "Well, why can't I `pip` install this?" The answer is: "We're kind of still working on it and it's not fully done."

> **Glyph Lefkowitz: 'I do think that Python will certainly keep growing in a variety of different backend capacities.'**

The answer should just be, of course, that you can *pip* install it and it shouldn't be harder than that. So that's where I hope the community will go, but I do think that Python will certainly keep growing in a variety of different backend capacities.

I also think that where we're headed as a language and an ecosystem is towards greater diversity. It's going to take us to some surprising places that I can't predict, but I would say that it looks like Python is going to be around for a really long time. I think that for now, where Python's going is data science. There are obviously a lot of people interested in data science right now.

Driscoll: Python is being used a lot in the AI and machine learning boom. Why do you think this is?

Lefkowitz: AI is a bit of a catch-all term that tends to mean whatever the most advanced areas in current computer science research are.

There was a time when the basic graph-traversal stuff that we take for granted was considered AI. At that time, Lisp was the big AI language, just because it was higher-level than average and easier for researchers to do quick prototypes with. I think Python has largely replaced it in the general sense because, in addition to being similarly high-level, it has an excellent third-party library ecosystem, and a great integration story for operating system facilities.

Lispers will object, so I should make it clear that I'm not making a precise statement about Python's position in a hierarchy of expressiveness, just saying that both Python and Lisp are in the same class of language, with things like garbage collection, memory safety, modules, namespaces and high-level data structures.

In the more specific sense of machine learning, which is what more people mean when they say AI these days, I think there are more specific answers. The existence of NumPy and its accompanying ecosystem allows for a very research-friendly mix of high-level stuff, with very high-performance number-crunching. Machine learning is nothing if not very intense number-crunching.

> **Glyph Lefkowitz: 'The Python community's focus on providing friendly introductions... to non-programmers, has really increased its adoption in the sister disciplines of data science and scientific computing.'**

The Python community's focus on providing friendly introductions and ecosystem support to non-programmers, has really increased its adoption in the sister disciplines of data science and scientific computing. Countless working statisticians, astronomers, biologists, and business analysts have become Python programmers and have improved the tooling. Programming is fundamentally a social activity and Python's community has acknowledged this more than any other language except JavaScript.

Machine learning is a particularly integration-heavy discipline, in the sense that any AI/machine learning system is going to need to ingest large amounts of data from real-world sources as training data, or system input, so Python's broad library ecosystem means that it is often well-positioned to access and transform that data.

Driscoll: What could be done to make Python a better language for AI and machine learning?

Lefkowitz: Using more PyPy. Right now, the data science/machine learning ecosystem in Python is very focused around the CPython runtime, which is unfortunate.

This means that new tools are often created without testing on PyPy, which means that when they have performance bottlenecks, rewrites of core logic in C (or, if you're lucky, Cython) are an inevitable part of any significant project.

> **Glyph Lefkowitz: 'Right now the data science/ machine learning ecosystem in Python is very focused around the CPython runtime, which is unfortunate.'**

This is largely a social problem and the technical challenges preventing some parts of the current Python AI/machine learning infrastructure from running, or running well, on PyPy are not significant in terms of the resources they would take to fix if their maintainers cared. But, from the perspective of someone uninvolved with those projects, who is starting a project and trying to use PyPy, it's just one inscrutable failure after another in some code you don't know anything about.

This is true in several fields of Python's application and I just wish that more folks would think of Python as a language that can be very fast, and competitive with Java or even C++, and plan accordingly when evaluating their testing matrix.

> **Glyph Lefkowitz: 'I just wish that more folks would think of Python as a language that can be very fast, and competitive with Java or even C++.'**

Driscoll: What changes would you like to see in future Python releases?

Lefkowitz: My main wish is for there to be some good defaults for getting new projects set up.

For example, today you have to know that when you install Python, you also need to install `pip`, and then you also need to create a `virtualenv`, but all of these steps are optional. You also have to hand-create a `setup.py` to describe your project, then learn about building wheels, specifying dependencies and so on.

What I'd like to see is Python presenting an integrated view of best practices, that makes it harder to get lost in the weeds of installing stuff. This could be just having a `new project` button, so that a Python project would look like any other kind of document to a user just getting started. Also, Python could look more like an app, even if that app required lots of command-line use.

Secondary to that, I'd like to see tools that make it easier for library authors to protect private implementation details from accidental breakage. For example, you can import the stuff that the library has imported, rather than importing the stuff that the library is trying to define. Right now, upgrading Python libraries is extra risky, because every single user of every library might have made a mistake like this and be depending on a bug.

The tool that I want to make it easy for users to create projects would benefit a lot from coming with the language, but this type of boundary enforcement around modules would have to be built into the language. It would be extremely hard to build it in the ecosystem.

Driscoll: So what do you think is the best thing about the Python community?

Lefkowitz: One of the things that I think is really good is the commitment to diversity. A lot of people think that this is a political thing or that there are different factions for pro-diversity and anti-diversity. Diversity is almost seen as taking away from the technical stuff somehow.

I can just share my own personal journey to becoming interested in diversity and social justice. I looked around a Twisted project and I said, "Why are we 100% dudes? What is going on here? What have we done to shut women out of this project?"

> **Glyph Lefkowitz: 'We were clearly missing out on half the talent the world had to offer.'**

I felt bad, but also that we were clearly missing out on half the talent the world had to offer in just the most obvious way. We were also all white and there are lots of people of color who also have talent to offer. They weren't showing up. So there's certainly a degree of altruistic impulses, but I also think that many people inside the Python community have accepted that this is a real skills gap issue.

If we don't get a diverse group of people working on our stuff, and getting involved in our community, then we're not going to make software that's useful to a lot of the world. We're going to be missing out on a lot of talent and we're going to be missing out on a lot of interesting voices that will challenge us, and make us a more interesting community.

> **Glyph Lefkowitz: 'If we don't get a diverse group of people working on our stuff... then we're not going to make software that's useful.'**

So when we talked earlier about the technical directions that the Python community has been moving in, those directions are aided by this pursuit of diversity. I believe that one of the reasons that Python is popular in life sciences is that it has a different demographic breakdown than the rest of the tech industry. I think Python has made real inroads there, in large part because people look at the Python community and are not scared off. It's not an intimidating or exclusionary type of environment.

> **Glyph Lefkowitz: 'The Python community is not perfect. We still have a long way to go.'**

Now that said, I felt a little weird commenting on this because I also feel that the Python community is not perfect. We still have a long way to go. The tech industry overall is highlighting women, just because that's the most obvious demographic disparity, but there are also lots of other underrepresented groups.

When you look at the representation of women throughout the software industry, you've got about 25 to 30%, depending on how it's measured. Then you look at the open source community and it's more like 5% women, which is a lot better than it was a couple of years ago, when it was about 1%.

The Python community is considerably better than that, but still when you look at people who are actively participating in projects, it's not even really hitting the industry average, let alone the overall demographic average.

Driscoll: How can the Python community encourage more diversity?

Lefkowitz: I think we still have a long way to go, but the fact that the Python community has, in the large part, acknowledged the real problem that's affecting a lot of aspects of technology is important. Diversity is an issue that's affecting the culture around technology.

> **Glyph Lefkowitz: 'Diversity is an issue that's affecting the culture around technology.'**

You have other communities, like Clojure or Erlang, which have fantastic technology on offer, but they don't really care about the diversity problem. You can see that reflected in a monoculture among their thinking and the lack of success becoming more popular.

I think a community which is largely following in Python's footsteps is Rust. Despite it being extremely low-level and somewhat tedious to write, they do have some great ideas in that language. As a result of being more inclusive and thoughtful about the way the community is organized, Rust is skyrocketing in popularity from very far down on the list of languages.

> **Glyph Lefkowitz: 'I think that the inclusiveness of the Python community is definitely the best thing about it.'**

So I think that the inclusiveness of the Python community is definitely the best thing about it. That is not just a comment on its political orientation, but a comment on its ability to produce interesting technology in the future.

I think that Python has endured by being friendly. It's open to lots of people from new and different communities. I don't know how to predict the future really, because it's going to depend on who shows up next.

Driscoll: Thank you, Glyph Lefkowitz.

5

Doug Hellmann

Doug Hellmann is an American software developer and author. He is a fellow of the Python Software Foundation (PSF) and served as communications director for almost two years. Doug was a columnist for the Python Magazine, before becoming editor-in-chief. He also created and sustained the popular Python Module of the Week blog, which was compiled and published in his book, *The Python 3 Standard Library by Example*. Doug works as a senior principal software engineer at Red Hat, where he focuses on community leadership and achieving long-term sustainability for OpenStack.

Discussion themes: OpenStack, virtualenvwrapper, v2.7/v3.x.

Catch up with Doug Hellmann here: @doughellman

Mike Driscoll: Why did you become a programmer, Doug?

Doug Hellmann: I got interested in computers when I was pretty young, through some summer programs that my local school system ran at the time. I enjoyed programming, and learning about how computers work, so I decided to pursue a CS degree in college. The work we did in school really reinforced for me that programming was something I could enjoy doing for a living.

Driscoll: Why Python? What makes Python special to you?

Hellmann: I was first introduced to Python around 1997, when I was working in a tools and build management group for a GIS software company called ERDAS.

We needed to build some tools to help manage the builds on several UNIX platforms, as well as Windows NT and 95. We had a lot of Makefiles and shell scripts, but they weren't especially portable. The more I used Python, the more I was able to find new ways to use it.

> **Doug Hellmann: 'The more I used Python, the more I was able to find new ways to use it.'**

After first learning Python, I remember being simultaneously happy that I had found a new tool language that was so easy to use, and sad that the company I was working with didn't let us use it for 'real work' at the time!

Driscoll: Doug, you went on to become the technical editor for Python Magazine, which I used to really enjoy. I've always wondered how Python Magazine got started...and why did it then stop?

Hellmann: Python Magazine began with Brian Jones as the first editor-in-chief.

Brian pitched the idea to MTA, the publishers. They had been focused on the PHP community, but agreed that it seemed like the Python community could also support a magazine.

Was that the right call? Well, we did okay for a while, but I think the timing was poor for a new paid print publication to launch. An e-zine might work better, today, but it's a tough industry.

Driscoll: What made you also start the tremendously successful 'Python Module of the Week' series, Doug? What's driven you to carry on writing PyMOTW for more than ten years now?

Hellmann: Yes, it has been over ten years. I started the PyMOTW blog series (`https://pymotw.com`) in 2007 as a way to push myself to write on a regular basis. I decided a theme would make it easier to find topics to write about, and writing once a week seemed like a good goal.

The interest from the rest of the community grew slowly over time, but feedback was mostly positive. I'm sure I would have stopped early on if it wasn't for all of the feedback and support that everyone has given me.

Driscoll: How did your book come about, Doug?

Hellmann: At a PyCon a couple of years into the project, Mark Ramm introduced me to Debra Williams Cauley, an editor from Pearson. I pitched the idea of cleaning up the blog posts and turning the series into a book. Debra helped me to figure out how to structure it to make it work in that format. The whole team at Pearson has been great to work with.

> **Doug Hellmann: 'The Python 3 Standard Library contains hundreds of modules for interacting with the operating system, interpreter, and internet.'**

Driscoll: Your book is incredibly helpful to Python developers. So what do you think new Python programmers should do once they've learned the basics?

Hellmann: I encourage folks to set a goal by picking a problem that they want to solve for themselves. That gives them a framework for learning things like how to break down a project into pieces that can be implemented one at a time, which in turn helps them to focus on learning one skill at a time.

At PyOhio 2015, I talked about one of my own projects as an example of this. Of course, not all projects need to be as complex as the Smiley example:

`https://doughellmann.com/blog/2015/08/02/pyohio-talk-on-smiley-and-iterative-development/`

Every programmer builds little throw-away tool scripts as well as more complicated reusable projects, and all of them are an opportunity to learn something new.

> **Doug Hellmann: 'Every programmer builds little throw-away tool scripts as well as more complicated reusable projects, and all of them are an opportunity to learn something new.'**

Another good way to learn is to attend a local meetup, and talk to other programmers. The Atlanta Python meetup group tries to maintain a good mix of introductory and more advanced talks to help encourage folks with a range of skills to attend our meetings. Sometimes the most informative part of the evening is the Q&A after a talk, or the discussions during breaks, when you have the chance to ask for more detail or clarification.

Driscoll: What active projects are you involved in today Doug?

Hellmann: For the past five years I've been working on various aspects of OpenStack. Aside from the cloud management software itself, we've produced some interesting tools like the pbr library, to help with packaging.

Driscoll: So how did you get started as an OpenStack developer?

Hellmann: I started working on OpenStack at DreamHost. I had known Jonathan LaCour, the VP of engineering, through the Atlanta Python meetup for a few years and the timing worked out well when he needed someone, and I was interested in changing jobs. We had a small team in the Atlanta area, and we all helped each other to bootstrap into the OpenStack community.

> **Doug Hellmann: 'I had known Jonathan LaCour, VP of Engineering, through the Atlanta Python meetup for a few years...'**

Driscoll: So the power of meetups was really in action there! What are your goals for OpenStack at the moment?

Hellmann: I have a very flexible mandate from Red Hat to work on what's needed to keep the OpenStack community healthy.

I serve on the Technical Committee, which is our elected governing body. We try to guide the project, and help to bring the large contributor base to some level of consensus when we have major decisions to make.

> **Doug Hellmann: 'I have a very flexible mandate from Red Hat to work on what's needed to keep the OpenStack community healthy.'**

I have also served as team lead for the Oslo team, which manages the set of common libraries shared between the various OpenStack services. We try to build the libraries to be as reusable as possible, but sometimes we need to share code within OpenStack that isn't going to be that useful to anyone else.

I've also worked on the release tools, extending the pipeline to make the release process scale from a highly manual process for five projects, to a highly automated process supporting around 350 different deliverables. I've built some tools like `reno`, our release note management program, and I jump in on other initiatives where help is needed.

Driscoll: So, regarding some of the tools that you've created, what was your inspiration for creating `virtualenvwrapper`?

Hellmann: While I was working as a technical editor and later editor-in-chief for Python Magazine, I ended up needing to manage a lot of different `virtualenv`'s. Each author provided instructions for installing the tools they used for their articles, and I wanted to be able to test out the code.

I started writing a few aliases to manage environments easily, and the project grew organically from there. My workflow has changed significantly since I've been so focused on OpenStack, so I haven't been contributing to `virtualenvwrapper` as much as I used to. I'm happy to have Jason Myers taking over as the lead maintainer on the project these days.

Driscoll: So while you were creating `virtualenvwrapper`, can you tell us what you learned?

Hellmann: Sure, I can actually think of three things that I learned while I was creating `virtualenvwrapper`.

First of all I learned how contributions come from surprising directions. Doug Latornell provided the original patches to support ksh. I had no idea that anyone would be interested in supporting ksh, so I hadn't thought beyond Bash. I think he was using `virtualenvwrapper` on an AIX system at that point, though, and his patches were easy to integrate and support once they merged.

The second thing I learned was that it's important to keep it fun. For instance, I created the following site just because of a Tweet from Alex Gaynor:

`https://bitbucket.org/dhellmann/virtualenvwrapper.alex`

"The `virtualenvwrapper.alex` installs aliases for typos related to common `virtualenvwrapper` commands. Really. It exists because Alex Gaynor asked nicely."

The third learning point that I have to offer is that you can't please everyone all of the time. So `virtualenvwrapper` supports plugins to enable folks to share their extensions, but there is now an entire category of similar tools like `pyenv`, `vex`, and others where the operating model is very different. That's great! As I said, my own workflow has changed enough that I don't rely on `virtualenvwrapper` so much anymore, either.

Driscoll: So if you could start `virtualenvwrapper` from scratch, what would you do differently?

Hellmann: I would now build it on Python 3's `venv` instead of `virtualenv` and today I would design it as a single main command that took subcommands.

Driscoll: What are you most excited about in Python today?

Hellmann: I have always been most excited about the vibrant community. As more people discover Python, or apply it in new areas, that community keeps expanding.

Mike Driscoll: What are your thoughts on the long life of Python 2.7?

Hellmann: The long lifetime for Python 2.7 recognizes the reality that rewriting functional software based on backwards-incompatible upstream changes isn't a high priority for most companies.

I encourage people to use the latest version of Python 3 that is available on their deployment platform for all new projects. I also advise them to carefully reconsider porting their remaining legacy applications now that most actively maintained libraries support Python 3.

Driscoll: What changes would you like to see in future Python releases?

Hellmann: I am most interested in the work related to packaging right now. Those changes will not go into Python itself, but into tools like `setuptools`, `twine`, `wheel`, `pip`, and `warehouse`. Simplifying the process of packaging and distributing Python packages will help all of our users.

Driscoll: Thank you, Doug Hellmann.

6

MASSIMO DI PIERRO

Massimo Di Pierro is an Italian web developer, data science expert, and lecturer. For the last 15 years, Massimo has been a professor for the School of Computing at DePaul University in Chicago. He is the inventor and lead developer of web2py, an open source web application framework written in Python. Massimo is a regular contributor to open source Python projects around the world and has published three books on Python, including *Annotated Algorithms in Python*. His active work in the Python community has seen him elected a member of the Python Software Foundation (PSF).

Discussion themes: web2py, Python books, v2.7/v3.x.
Catch up with Massimo Di Pierro here: @mdipierro

Mike Driscoll: How did you become a computer programmer?

Massimo Di Pierro: So I am a physicist, but I actually started computer programming when I was in middle school. My dad had the IBM PC at home. He was a COBOL programmer and he was mostly working with accounting software.

When I was 13 years old, my dad gave a lecture on COBOL. I went with him and he thought I was just tagging along, but I understood what he was saying and something clicked. My dad then got me a Commodore 64 and I started programming in BASIC first, and Pascal later.

Driscoll: So how did you get into the Python language?

Di Pierro: That was much later. I was doing my Ph.D. in the UK and I was mostly programming in Fortran, C, and C++. My work was on lattice quantum chromodynamics and my machine was a Cray T3E. That was when I started learning Python. At the time, it was mostly used as a tool to automate the processing of file and scripting maintenance tasks. By 2004, it had become my favorite language.

Driscoll: Was there some epiphany that made you decide that Python was your favorite language, or were you just using the language so much?

Di Pierro: So, at the time, a lot of the libraries that exist today were either not available, or not as mature.

The thing that I really liked about Python was that I could do introspection: I could ask a function what its arguments were. So using Python, I could write code that would understand itself to some extent.

> **Di Pierro: 'Using Python, I could write code that would understand itself to some extent.'**

I remember doing something similar in BASIC many years before, but I could not easily do that in a language like C++. I really liked the idea of writing a program that could rewrite itself. For example, I have written a library called OCL that allows me to decorate some simple functions in Python, and they get converted at runtime, in C or OpenCL, and run at a higher speed (it uses PyOpenCL).

Driscoll: So what made you create web2py?

Di Pierro: So web2py started in 2007. At that time, the two most popular Python frameworks were Django and TurboGears. I had two needs: I wanted to teach web development in the model-view-controller architecture, and for myself I needed to build some web apps.

I was evaluating Django and TurboGears, and I had been using Django for some time. I had built a content management system for the United Nations in Django, as pro bono work with the university. So I knew Django pretty well, but I thought that Django was verbose and kind of difficult to teach as a first framework.

In order to be able to prime in Django for example, you needed to have some familiarity with the Bash shell and some system administration tools. A lot of my students at that time did not have that experience. So I wanted to teach web development in Python, but for me to go through all the tools to get to that point was too much work. I needed a framework that would download a file, start, and do everything through the web interface.

> **Di Pierro: 'I needed a framework that would download a file, start, and do everything through the web interface.'**

I also worked in TurboGears, which in many ways I liked better than Django. But TurboGears was going through a big transition. It was a framework assembled out of components, and a lot of the components were being replaced, because they were not being maintained.

TurboGears did not appear to have a stable API and therefore it was not suitable for me as a teaching tool. So I decided to apply what I had learned, and build a framework which, in my opinion, was simpler to start with. I never thought that framework would become as popular as it did.

> **Di Pierro: 'I decided to apply what I had learned, and build a framework which, in my opinion, was simpler to start with.'**

Driscoll: So what do you consider to be the most important lesson that you learned while you were creating web2py?

Di Pierro: The most important lesson that I learned was the importance of building a community. I got to know a lot of people by working with them remotely, although many of them I have still never met.

When I started web2py I was not familiar with collaboration tools like Git. The first version of web2py used Launchpad. I remember having interactions where people just sent me emails offering their help or making suggestions. I was not prepared for that.

> **Di Pierro: 'I still consider it a critical skill being able to collaborate with people remotely, even if you don't know them personally.'**

I didn't know exactly how to handle collaboration for many years. Today, I still consider it a critical skill being able to collaborate with people remotely, even if you don't know them personally. I mean, eventually I got to know them and trust them a lot. Some of the people I trust the most are people I met through web2py.

Driscoll: Are there any features that you've seen in FaaS or Django that you think would be good in web2py?

Di Pierro: web2py owes a lot to Django, as many ideas came from it, as well as from other frameworks. Yet, we added into web2py many features that Django did not have at the time. For example, stronger default security settings, like always escaping strings by default. The frameworks have very different philosophies.

There are many projects that use Django and each one has a different name and its own maintainers. They are very advanced and very well maintained. In web2py, we try to keep everything in one package, so that we don't have a big ecosystem outside of the framework.

> **Di Pierro: 'web2py owes a lot to Django, as many ideas came from it, as well as from other frameworks.'**

There are many ideas from web2py that originated in other frameworks, but I believe that we improved on some of those ideas. For example, the mechanism for form generation and processing in web2py is not unique but, when it was developed, it was better than the competition.

The model-view-controller design architecture was mostly taken from Django and the URL mapping was also very similar. For the latter, we gave it default routing rules, like in Ruby on Rails. For the template language, we decided that we didn't want a domain-specific language. Instead, we wanted pure Python in templates, which is kind of the same model as the ERB template language in Ruby on Rails, but using the Python language.

There are other features, that were added later in web2py that were also inspired by other frameworks. For example, one thing I liked from Flask was this idea of thread-local variables. So thread-local would allow any module to access the current request object, the current response object, or the current session, even if the code was rooted in a module which was imported from somewhere else. I liked the way Flask handled that.

So there are definitely many ideas that came from other frameworks and I think there's been a lot of learning from each other. Not everybody admits that, but I'm happy to admit it.

> **Di Pierro: 'There's been a lot of learning from each other. Not everybody admits that, but I'm happy to admit it.'**

Driscoll: So I saw that you started self-publishing books. How did that happen?

Di Pierro: I'm an academic, so I'm supposed to write papers and write books. Because I was writing documentation for software, it was extremely important for me to have the ability to update the content of a book quickly. Self-publishing allows that.

I really believe in open source, not just for code, but in general for educational content. I self-publish my books almost at cost and I make them available for free download. For me, making the content up-to-date and available quickly is the priority.

Moreover, if I write a book, then it is because I want people to read it, not because I think there is a profit to be made. In the end, the validation of the content comes from the readers and not from the publisher. So I found that self-publishing was ideal for me. That said, once you're done with a book, then you don't want to touch it too much. Instead, you want to write another book!

Driscoll: Did you have any challenges that you needed to overcome when you were writing your books?

Di Pierro: Well, first of all, I'm not a native English speaker. So I can write, but I tend to make a lot of mistakes. It takes me forever to review things and make sure that they are fixed.

> **Di Pierro: 'Even if I consider myself an expert, that does not mean that I know everything about a subject.'**

Another challenge is that even if I consider myself an expert, that does not mean that I know everything about a subject. I always have a process, which is to write the code first. Then I look at the code and I turn the code into a paper or a book. In that way, I manage to make the text consistent with the code examples. If you change the code after you've written the text, then sometimes the text gets out of sync, so I really try to make sure that my examples are as good and as complete as possible.

One challenge surrounding the book *web2py* was that I had a lot of people submitting pull requests to the book on GitHub. They initially contributed by making small corrections, but now sometimes they contribute quite substantially.

Keeping track of contributors was difficult, because I knew their GitHub names, but I couldn't acknowledge them as people properly. People always send me code, but they never submit the pull request in the acknowledgements section. It's work for me to figure out who these people are to acknowledge them.

Driscoll: So as a scientist, or a teacher, how do you see Python helping the scientific community?

Di Pierro: I can see that Python has been growing a lot and especially within the scientific community. In particular, I've seen growth with all of the machine learning stuff that's been coming out, such as sklearn, TensorFlow, and Keras.

I remember when I started teaching 15 years ago, people didn't know what Python was. Some colleagues were objecting to a switch from Java to Python as the primary teaching language. Python was considered by many to be "only a scripting language" and something very specialized.

> **Di Pierro: 'Python was considered by many to be "only a scripting language" and something very specialized.'**

Today, in almost every class we teach, whether it's a neural network class, a machine learning class, or a data analysis class, almost everybody uses Python. So things have really changed a lot in that respect.

> **Di Pierro: 'The major problem I see is that the relation between Python 2 and Python 3 is still an issue.'**

The major problem I see is that the relation between Python 2 and Python 3 is still an issue. At DePaul University, we use Python 3 almost everywhere, whereas the industry still uses mostly Python 2 everywhere, which is a problem sometimes.

Another issue is that very few people use the new async logic that is available in Python 3. I think Python's new async logic is really powerful, but it's not as friendly as JavaScript's async logic. People who really like event-driven async programming tend to prefer JavaScript (and Node.js) over Python.

> **Di Pierro: 'I think Python's new async logic is really powerful, but it's not as friendly as JavaScript's async logic.'**

Driscoll: I'm actually a little bit concerned about these other companies that are starting to support Python 2. What do you think is going to happen to these splinter groups, that are following Anaconda or Intel, if they continue to support Python 2 instead of 3?

Di Pierro: Well, I don't argue about the fact that Python 3 is a better language than Python 2, but I think that migration from Python 2 to Python 3 is difficult. It cannot be completely automated and often it requires understanding the code. People do not want to touch things that currently work.

> **Di Pierro: 'I don't argue about the fact that Python 3 is a better language than Python 2, but I think that migration from Python 2 to Python 3 is difficult.'**

For example, the `str` function in Python 2 converts to a string of bytes, but in Python 3, it converts to Unicode. So this makes it impossible to switch from Python 2 to Python 3, without actually going through the code and understanding what type of input is being passed to the function, and what kind of output is expected.

A naïve conversion may work very well as long as you don't have any strange characters in your input (like byte sequences that do not map into Unicode). When that happens, you don't know if the code is doing what it was supposed to do originally or not. Consider banks, for example. They have huge codebases in Python, which have been developed and tested over many years. They are not going to switch easily because it is difficult to justify that cost. Consider this: some banks still use COBOL.

There are tools to help with the transition from Python 2 to Python 3. I'm not really an expert on those tools, so a lot of the problems I see may have a solution that I'm not aware of. But I still found that each time I had to convert code, this process was not as straightforward as I would like.

Driscoll: Do you see Python having any challenges in its adoption by data science?

Di Pierro: I think that data scientists love Python. The major competitor is R and I get the impression that R is more popular among economists and statisticians. But I don't think R is more popular because it's better, only because it has been around longer and it is more focused.

R has been around for a long time and people know what they can do with R. The people who know the language well don't see the need to learn something different. R has always been focused on data science specifically, so people in that community are more familiar with that language.

> **Di Pierro: 'I see Python being adopted more and more and eventually becoming more popular than R for data science.'**

I would compare R not so much with Python as a language, but with the pandas library. I think that Python plus pandas makes a compelling case in a comparison with R. That, in fact, is what I am using right now in a machine learning class. But I see Python being adopted more and more and eventually becoming more popular than R for data science. I've no doubt that will happen.

Driscoll: Thank you, Massimo Di Pierro.

7

ALEX MARTELLI

Alex Martelli is an Italian computer engineer. He is the author of the first two editions of *Python in a Nutshell* and the co-author of the first two editions of *Python Cookbook* and the third edition of *Python in a Nutshell.* Alex is a fellow of the Python Software Foundation (PSF) and the winner of both the 2002 Activators' Choice Award and the 2006 Frank Willison Memorial Award for contributions to the Python community. Since 2005, he has worked for Google, and today he is a senior staff engineer and tech lead of the team providing community support for Google Cloud Platform. Alex is an active contributor to Stack Overflow and a frequent speaker at technical conferences.

Discussion themes: Python books, v2.7/v3.x,
Python at Google.
Catch up with Alex Martelli here: @aleaxi

Mike Driscoll: Could you give us a little background information about yourself?

Alex Martelli: I graduated in electrical engineering back in my home country, Italy. I then started looking around for jobs where I could design integrated circuits. Designing other kinds of systems sounded cool, but integrated circuits were where it was at.

At the time, most really interesting design was being done by American firms, so I ended up with my very first job being in America, specifically with Texas Instruments (TI), which is still around.

TI was very prominent, with both consumer products and a lot of very interesting chips. We apparently weren't very compatible though, because the style of working in TI included starting a lot of projects and terminating them very abruptly. I found myself in the terminated project teams over and over again.

> **Alex Martelli: 'I found myself in the terminated project teams over and over again.'**

I can't blame TI for that. They were trying to minimize disruption in engineers' lives, and as the youngest guy, and an immigrant, I obviously had no roots in any specific place. In less than a year, I ended up working in Dallas, Austin, Houston and Lubbock. That's four different labs in less than a year!

It was a bit stressful, so I restarted talks with IBM Research that I had blocked when I got the interesting offer from TI. It's not widely known, but IBM used to make some of the most innovative integrated circuits in the business, especially at research level, where they wouldn't be mass-produced, but be proofs of concept. IBM still has incredible technology in the field.

I remember around that time, IBM got a Nobel Prize for spelling out the word IBM in single atoms, with a very novel use of an electron microscope to place atoms, rather than observe them. It still strikes me as a science fiction event.

IBM, at some point, decided that it wanted a research lab in Italy, specifically Rome, and asked for volunteers. Of course, I volunteered. It would give me an interesting perspective and get me back to my home country, with better cappuccinos and pasta being the main attractions! So I found myself back in Italy in the 80s and my career kept developing from there.

Driscoll: How did you end up becoming a computer programmer?

Martelli: So that was at IBM. We had just finished developing this prototype image processing machine which, for the time, was incredible. It had dedicated chips, a big frame buffer and a monitor that cost a fortune at the time (though it would be considered nothing special nowadays).

> **Alex Martelli: 'We had just finished developing this prototype image processing machine which, for the time, was incredible.'**

At the celebration for the successful launch of our prototype, a director came up to me and said, "Congratulations to you and all the team. It's a pity that the prototype will now be gathering dust in a corner." To which I replied, "Why should it gather dust in a corner? We have at IBM Research a lot of scientists in all sorts of disciplines, and there's demand from astronomers to geologists."

"Yeah right," he said, "but your device doesn't support the programming languages scientists use, such as Fortran and APL. To use the device, you need to write a channel program." The geologists and astronomers just didn't do those. It would require a substantial software project to build all of the interfaces and libraries they needed.

I then said, "Well, can't we put together a small team to build that software?" So he challenged me: "How many people do you think it would need?"

I was really keen to have 'my' machine see use, rather than gather dust, so I shot very low. I said, "Maybe three?"

He replied, "Okay, I can put in the people. So you go and put together the team. Show me something working in six months."

That's how you get to be a director at IBM I imagine. Not exactly by setting low bars. So I had to improvise becoming a small-level manager (I think technical lead is the correct term). I needed to teach myself enough software to start writing the channel programs, incorporating them into libraries, and finding out what algorithms they wanted in a library, especially those which could be accelerated by this very powerful peripheral.

Driscoll: So did you succeed?

Martelli: After six months, we had a proof of concept that barely worked, but we were given the go-ahead to continue. In the end, it took a couple of years, but we did deliver working libraries for APL and Fortran as desired. That was actually very significant.

> **Alex Martelli: 'We did deliver working libraries for APL and Fortran as desired. That was actually very significant.'**

It made this beautiful piece of hardware meaningful. It was actually usable by scientists and other programmers for powerful image processing and visualization. Without the intermediate software, they wouldn't teach themselves the assembly programming and channel programming to do that.

The problem, from my viewpoint, was that for over two years, I had done no hardware design at all. I had not even followed what was going on in the field. Hardware design, especially at an integrated circuit level, tended to get about a revolution per year, at the time. So if you weren't very much on top of the game, then you lost track.

Driscoll: Is that why you moved towards software?

Martelli: Well, I had to realize that despite my years of experience, I could be run circles around by any bright guy fresh out of college, with the latest technologies and tools under his fingers.

On the other hand, I also had to realize that even the most simple kind of management and software was a huge added value to the stuff that I really wanted to do, which was to make cool systems with dedicated integrated circuits.

So, on the slippery slope a few years later, I had to admit that I wasn't actually able to design decent modern hardware anymore. It was more and more software and management all the way. I think there are a lot of people in similar situations, who start out on the hardware side and then gradually realize that their hardware isn't really solving problems.

> **Alex Martelli: 'A lot of people...start out on the hardware side and then gradually realize that their hardware isn't really solving problems.'**

My daughter is in a similar situation now. She's got a Ph.D. in telecommunication engineering (advanced radio systems) and she was very keen to focus on hardware. Nowadays, her working days tend to be about three-quarters software. That's because essentially, all networking, more and more down to the lower levels, is software-driven.

You don't design a specialized antenna, which works by itself, with no intelligence and no software. These days, your apparatus has to have a dazzling array of antennas and enough intelligence to find out which ones should be activated at some point, based on the signal quality. That is far beyond what radio meant back when I graduated, but it's very much the software networking of today.

Driscoll: So how did you end up getting into Python itself?

Martelli: Oh, that's a different funny story. Years after my first introduction to the beguiling world of software, I had written an experimental system, on my own time and using my own equipment, to develop certain ideas about the game of contract bridge.

Contract bridge was invented in the 1920s by Harold Vanderbilt. Until about the time that I started dabbling with the game, there was little mathematical theory on it. There was one major exception: Émile Borel, the great mathematician, wrote a book on the mathematical theory of bridge.

By the time that I came along, computers had become strong, powerful and cheap enough to be used for recreational things, without necessarily a big payoff. So I resurrected an idea that had been first expressed as a thought experiment in the 1930s, and put it into practice on my new PC.

> **Alex Martelli: 'I resurrected an idea that had been first expressed as a thought experiment in the 1930s.'**

Perhaps I acted like a typical hardware guy turned to software, because my solution wasn't exactly organized as a nice programming system; it was a horrid mix of so many programming languages. I lost count from Modula-3 to Perl, and from Visual Basic to Scheme, but the whole thing worked!

Driscoll: Did the program play a lot of games successfully?

Martelli: The program actually played each hand a million times and recorded the results. It confirmed the incredible intuition of Ely Culbertson, who was the brightest figure of bridge back in the 1920s and 1930s.

So I wrote everything up as a research paper and submitted it to the most prestigious magazine in the field: The Bridge World. The editor was enthusiastic and worked with me to vastly improve the paper. My research was published in January and February of the year 2000, in The Bridge World.

After that, I started getting communications from bridge players, including champions, asking me, "Hey, can you apply your theory and your method to this particular problem I'm struggling with?"

I was quite happy to accommodate them, except that the whole thing was so fragile and each time I changed a comma here, something broke over there. It was a mess! So I decided, despite it being usually considered a trap, that the whole system needed to be rewritten. I wanted it to be in, as much as possible, a single language, but exactly which single language was a real problem!

Driscoll: So did you find the language that you were looking for?

Martelli: The only language with enough power would have been Lisp. I honestly always had a strong predilection for Scheme, but maybe that had something to do with the hardware background of Scheme itself.

The problem was that the free editions that I could get, just didn't have enough libraries for all of the auxiliary tasks that I needed to do. It was a personal project and I was already pouring a lot of hours into it, but I didn't want to spend money as well. A colleague said, "Hey, you should try this brand-new language that's coming out. It's all the rage and it's known as Python."

> **Alex Martelli: 'A colleague said, "Hey, you should try this brand-new language that's coming out. It's all the rage and it's known as Python."'**

I said, "Oh, come on! I know at least a dozen languages. The last thing I need is to learn yet another!" He kept insisting, and I had a lot of respect for this guy, so I finally gave in and gave it a try. I set myself a little task to solve with this brand-new language, to see how far along I got.

> **Alex Martelli: 'I said, "Oh, come on! I know at least a dozen languages. The last thing I need is to learn yet another!"'**

Another thing that I didn't know much about in the late 1990s was the newfangled 'web'. It seemed interesting, so I decided to develop a website. I taught myself the web technologies, and the Python programming language, all within a weekend! As I said, you have to be somewhat ambitious in this field if you want to get anything done!

I started hacking on a Friday night and kept looking at the manual. At some point, I started looking much less at the manual, because if I just guessed how Python would work by analogy with how it worked elsewhere, then I was right more than 90% of the time. The language seemed to be designed just for my brain and worked exactly the way that my brain did.

> **Alex Martelli: 'That language seemed to be designed just for my brain and worked exactly the way that my brain did.'**

By early Saturday afternoon, I was done. I had a working CGI and web application that was computing the conditional probabilities of the division of suits in the game of contract bridge! Now, what could I do with the rest of the weekend?

I said, "I know, it's good, but it's only in Italian, and this may be interesting for readers in other languages. Let me make a multilingual version also in English or French, which are two other languages that I speak decently."

I realized that I needed a templating system. So I sniffed around for a templating system for Python without much success. I tried using Gofer and other tools of the time.

In the end, I decided to just write a templating system myself! I named it Yet Another Python Template Utility (YAPTU). By Sunday, it was working fine. So I packed it up, sent it to one of the places you distributed free software back then and I had my working website.

Driscoll: Did you get any interest?

Martelli: YAPTU actually attracted the attention of a guy who, at the time, happened to be doing the website for computer science at the University of California, Berkeley. He found YAPTU to be the best templating utility. He had already decided to use Python and so he made some improvements, then sent me a patch file. We started discussing things and then made friends.

> **Alex Martelli: 'We started discussing things and then made friends. The guy was Peter Norvig, who is now director of research at Google...'**

The guy was Peter Norvig, who is now director of research at Google and author of the bestselling programming book *Artificial Intelligence: A Modern Approach*. So Python was already starting to give me interesting connections at the time.

I tried pushing Python at work, but unfortunately without much success. Decision-making was in the hands of professional management and they knew that the future was Windows. Nothing else would survive, even though our programs were mostly intended for Unix workstations. It is true that these days, you can hardly buy a Unix workstation anywhere; it's all PCs with Linux or Windows. So in that sense, their vision was correct.

I didn't particularly like the fact that our programming languages were to be restricted to what Microsoft really wanted to support. I could never get official approval from top management. What I had to do was sneak Python into places where top management wouldn't notice, such as all the testing framework that we had, which was a hack of shell scripting `haha.bat` files.

That was before the .cmd era in Windows. They all became very useful and maintainable Python scripts, but it was a little unsatisfactory. I was spending all my working day debugging problems with Microsoft Fortran compiler, and then doing Python only in the ripples of time that I could steal here and there.

Driscoll: Slightly different topic, but how did you end up becoming an author of books on Python?

Martelli: I loved Python so much that I wanted to give back. I wanted to pay back the enormous gift that Guido van Rossum and everybody in the Python community had made to me, and everybody else, by developing this language.

What could I do? Well, there was this Usenet group called comp. lang.python, where people asked and answered questions. I have always had a knack for helping people out with technical questions. So, despite being a total newbie at the language, I started following. Whenever I noticed a question that I thought I could answer productively and constructively, I did so, and apparently with a lot of success!

> **Alex Martelli: 'I have always had a knack for helping people out with technical questions.'**

After just a few months, one of the old-timers of the Python community nicknamed me the Martelli Bot. Apparently, I was the third "bot" in the Python community. The point being that a huge amount of answers, which were always correct, qualified you as a bot. The guy who came up with the funny nickname, by the way, was Steve Holden, and I'm honored to say that he is one of my co-authors on my latest book: the third edition of *Python in a Nutshell.*

So anyway, this gained me street credibility in the Python community, and gave me the courage to get in touch with O'Reilly, noticing that there was no *Python in a Nutshell.* I said, "Hey, maybe I, perhaps with a more experienced co-author, could do something about it?"

They said, "Why do you need a co-author? Send us a sample chapter and a chapter plan." It developed from there.

> **Alex Martelli: 'I said, "Hey, maybe I, perhaps with a more experienced co-author, could do something about it?"'**

Driscoll: How did you find writing *Python Cookbook*?

Martelli: I had to take a little detour to co-write *Python Cookbook*, which had lost an author in the middle of early planning. It was fun because those were recipes from the community, but rephrased and adapted to actually usefully address the silly problem.

I contributed a lot of recipes on the ActiveState site as well. That was always fun! That was the equivalent of what would now be Stack Overflow. Questions and answers on technical issues about a specific topic have become well-served by Stack Overflow. I am very active on there: I'm the second top poster on the Python tag, and front page top 0.001% in reputation.

Incidentally, Stack Overflow's chief data scientist has just published a study about the popularity of programming languages, and how it changes with time based on tags and questions on Stack Overflow. The language with the fastest growing popularity is Python.

> **Alex Martelli: 'The forecast is that Python will become the most popular programming language and the one with the most active developers by early 2019.'**

The forecast is that Python will become the most popular programming language and the one with the most active developers by early 2019. Right now, it's just below Java and JavaScript, but it has passed everything else. Perl has disappeared, Ruby has disappeared, and C# is going down sharply. Only Java and JavaScript hold, but they're very flat, while Python is growing gangbusters.

> **Alex Martelli: 'Only Java and JavaScript hold, but they're very flat, while Python is growing gangbusters.'**

There is a 27% year-over-year growth in volume from a large base. I found that an interesting confirmation of the article earlier this year, from Spectrum Magazine, which proclaimed Python to be the most popular programming language this year.

That was based on a kind of subjective mix of very different indications, such as job offers, courses, and seminars. Whereas Stack Overflow's study was totally quantitative, totally objective, and just based on an incredibly large volume of data. They both came to exactly the same conclusion, except that Stack Overflow, of course, could quantify things much better and more precisely.

Driscoll: So could you describe anything that you've learned as an author of books?

Martelli: Well, first of all, no matter how well you think you know a language, you're probably wrong until you've written a couple of books in that language.

Ideally, you write with the cooperation of a patient, but firm, editor whose role is knowing the language, how it looks on the printed page, and how readers will absorb it.

Of course, English is my third language, so I never thought I had a particularly strong claim to having a command of it. But writing the books improved my understanding of exactly where, at least in written English, the problems are.

> **Alex Martelli: 'We'll keep using programming languages because of the inherent ambiguity, power, and difficulty of natural language.'**

It's amazing how powerful, rich, and difficult a tool natural language is. That's why we'll keep using programming languages: because of the inherent ambiguity, power, and difficulty of natural language. It's impossible to express things with absolute precision there.

Driscoll: Can you give an example?

Martelli: There was an anecdote I read once in the mailing list, about the risks of automation and computing. It was about a formally-defined system to route ambulances in a large urban area. So obviously it was literally a life-and-death task.

One of the things written down originally in natural language, and one of the constraints, was that when a call to the emergency number came, and the symptoms were identified as those of a stroke, an ambulance would be there in no more than 15 minutes (the maximum time that would still give you a good chance).

When the system was translated from natural language to proven correct programming, many things improved, except that there were a small, but worrying, number of cases where the ambulance had been scheduled and then it never showed up. So what happened was natural language just didn't map into formal logic.

> **Alex Martelli: 'Natural language just didn't map into formal logic.'**

Remember, it was an urban area, with traffic. Although an ambulance may have been blasting its sirens, it may still have been blocked for minutes and minutes. If this happened, when 15 minutes and 0.01 seconds had passed, the system deduced that the ambulance must already have arrived, because one of the postulates is that the ambulance always arrives in less than 15 minutes. So if an ambulance had already arrived, it would have been useless to send another one there too. This meant that it got rerouted.

In natural language, when we say that the ambulance must be there in less than 15 minutes, it's not a postulate because it's aspirational. What we really mean is it's absolutely important and by all means, please get the ambulance there that fast. It doesn't mean if you don't make it, then forget it because 15 minutes and 1 second is useless. It's undesirable, but better than nothing!

> **Alex Martelli: 'When you're in a programming language, your assertion is much simpler: you say what happens.'**

That's one tiny example of how natural language trips you up all the time. When you're in a programming language, your assertion is much simpler: you say what happens. If this isn't true, then you raise an exception. In natural language, there's so much background that you take for granted inevitably. This includes all common knowledge and what it means to be a human being in this culture.

Driscoll: So can you describe any of your most interesting interactions with the readers of your books?

Martelli: There have been a few! I'm probably thinking some of the most interesting ones were at work, where a colleague would come up to me and say, "So, I'm observing this strange behavior of..." some program or function they had just written.

I would take a look and spot the problem and help them to fix it. That was not so much based on me knowing Python any better, but on me having what I call *debugger eyes*. If you give me a page of text with one typo, for some reason I see the typo before I see the context of anything else. That is actually very helpful in programming, as it is in circuit design.

People used to say, "So, I always meant to ask you, are you the Alex Martelli who wrote that book?" It was kind of fun to say, "Yeah, that was me, in my copious spare time!"

> **Alex Martelli: 'You need kudos too, not just hard-core results.'**

That kind of made my day. It doesn't happen much anymore, because I've been at my current employer for 12 and a half years and people started to know me well enough. I mean it's not objectively productive, but hey! You need kudos too, not just hard-core results.

Driscoll: So do you think that Python 2.7 is dead?

Martelli: The third edition of *Python in a Nutshell* had a problem. I think we were right that Python 2.7 is far from dead.

Probably, the vast majority of the lines of Python currently deployed in production are Python 2.7, or other Python 2 versions, but those could move to 2.7 with hardly any effort. So obviously Python 2.7 is not going anywhere. It's actually probably going away in 2020 when the Python Software Foundation (PSF) officially stops supporting it (though I bet some entrepreneurs will offer ongoing support on a commercial basis). So it was crucial to also cover Python 3, 3.5, and 3.6, which were the recent releases and forthcoming releases as we planned and wrote the book.

> **Alex Martelli: 'Python 2.7 is far from dead.'**

It's too early right now to drop 2.7. So we have a book that covers both, and that makes it redundant if you only care about one of them. That's a problem that will go away by the next edition. Of course, we will be Python 3 something only and no 2.7 need apply.

A lot of stuff will remain in 2.7, probably because it's just too much of a code base. YouTube, for example, is essentially a Python system. There's millions of lines of super-optimized 2.7 and honestly, it's too hard to justify migrating it all from a business standpoint. We can't say let's rewrite X million lines of code, given the amount of optimization that has gone into YouTube for more than 10 years.

If rewriting were to slow YouTube down by 10%, can you quantify the cost of that, not just to Google, but to everybody, what with YouTube traffic making up so large a fraction of the internet's bandwidth? A 10% performance impact would severely make life worse for everybody. We can't afford that! So that'll go by other directions.

Driscoll: So what are some of Python's current problems as a language?

Martelli: So, if I had a magic wand and could go back to just before the first version of Python was published, and could make only one change, I would make it case insensitive.

> **Alex Martelli: 'Many of the best languages were case insensitive. That, to me, would be the greatest improvement.'**

I know since the C programming language came and dominated the scene, people think of case insensitive as weird. But from Fortran, to Pascal, to Ada, many of the best languages were case insensitive. That, to me, would be the greatest improvement.

You may not notice it so much in a Western culture, but the very concept of lowercase and uppercase is completely artificial. They are very much an artifact of our culture and of how we happen to have developed writing.

I loved the Macintosh file system, because when you created a file uppercase F-O-O (`FOO`), it preserved that case. But if you looked for lowercase `foo`, it still gave you the file. This is much more likely to be what you want as a human being.

> **Alex Martelli: 'Voice input has suddenly become an absolutely major approach to input.'**

Think of the voice recognition system. Voice input has suddenly become an absolutely major approach to input, because phones make it so much easier to speak to them, than to use their little keyboards. Having to maintain case distinction is a killer in that situation and shows up how totally artificial it is! Specifying uppercase or lowercase is just not natural pronunciation.

I find myself in a tiny minority wishing for case insensitive Python. It's true that just about every language that competes with Python is also case sensitive, so I guess it's a defect shared by just about every popular language today.

Something that Python does differently from other languages, and it would be a better language if it did it the same way, is one of the Python keywords. One of the most popular keywords is `def`, which is used to define a function. The problem is it's not a keyword and it's not a word. It doesn't mean anything! You know which language does it right there? JavaScript.

Driscoll: How does JavaScript differ?

Martelli: The equivalent keyword is `function`. I can't imagine why Python didn't use `function` to start with. It's so obvious! `function` is four more characters to type, but big deal! Any editor will AutoComplete for you, right?

I know technically speaking, saying `def foo` or `function foo` makes absolutely no difference. But I focus on the very little usability and understandability glitches.

> **Alex Martelli: 'Python is possibly the most usable and most understandable programming language there has ever been.'**

Python is possibly the most usable and most understandable programming language there has ever been. So those few places where it isn't kind of stand out more.

Python has only one kind of range and it's always going to be upper bound excluded, so it's much more consistent and much more clear. The places where a completely arbitrary word, such as `def`, is used is where the language could have been just as easily designed to use a readable word like `function`.

If people were completely terrified by the long word `function`, I would allow 'fun'. It's kind of a joke. After all, the language is named after Monty Python, so you can take 'fun' as an abbreviation of `function`, or simply select it because using Python is fun. It would still be better than `def`.

Driscoll: What do you think are Python's greatest strengths?

Martelli: I actually answered this one while dealing with the glitches. The strengths are the clarity and consistency of Python and the aspirational goal the language has, to have only one natural and obvious way to do things.

We can't quite get there of course, because for example, addition is commutative, so $a + b$ and $b + a$ are two ways to express the sum and Python cannot change that. But it's aspirational and it really helps to make somebody else's code much more readable to you on the first pass.

If they're at all a good Pythonista, or even a beginner, they will in most cases have chosen the one obvious way, because it does tend to be obvious. Where they haven't, and you show them what it would have been, it's much easier to convince them. So this kind of aspirational attempt to give one obvious way to express things is part of what makes the language so clear, so useful and so usable.

> **Alex Martelli: 'This kind of aspirational attempt to give one obvious way to express things is part of what makes the language so clear, so useful and so usable.'**

The fact that Python has extended to be used in just about every application niche you can think of, I believe descends from this clarity and conceptual simplicity. It really makes it easy to jump aboard.

Not everybody's brain will be such a perfect match for Python as mine is. I'm not saying every experienced programmer will teach themselves Python within one weekend, but it's a language where it can happen. Despite liking a lot of things in other languages, such as Rust, I can't imagine somebody doing the same in Rust in a weekend.

Driscoll: So where do you see Python going in the future?

Martelli: Everywhere! You know, one of the greatest scientific results of the last few years was the discovery of gravitational waves.

We had a couple of keynotes at the PyCon Italia conference. Python code was there as the common language to control all of the instrumentation responsible for gathering the data, which eventually showed that two black holes were slamming into each other and sending out those waves.

> **Alex Martelli: 'Python was there directing the data processing.'**

Incidentally, if I recall correctly, for several seconds just the waves sent by that one event produced more energy than all the rest of the universe was sending together. That's quite a phenomenon and Python was there directing the data processing. That is, overseeing all of the cleaning, analysis, and correlation of those measurements, to interpret them as an incredibly powerful short-duration event, incredibly far away. That clash happened billions of years ago and it's just the waves that are getting here right now. That's one example.

Science, of course, is fascinating because of that. More and more I end up chatting with big internet companies that still prefer to, for their core applications, use other programming languages. They do this because that's what the founder knew, and they have to accommodate Python only because they buy other companies.

A lot of purchases are going on in the high-tech field. More often than not, those other companies are using Python, because that's part of what makes them successful. They're twice, or three times more productive than the guys who are using lesser languages.

Driscoll: Do you think more companies will start using Python?

Martelli: Yes, any big company needs to adopt Python as one of the things admitted in its production systems. The launch of TensorFlow showed to me that Python will definitely be there at the forefront of machine learning and artificial intelligence.

Even if the internals are in super-optimized C++ and assembly language, at the application level the business logic will be in Python, because it makes no sense to spend the energy to remake it otherwise. So TensorFlow is Python at the core.

> **Alex Martelli: 'The launch of TensorFlow showed to me that Python will definitely be there at the forefront of machine learning and artificial intelligence.'**

I cannot imagine niches where Python will never be. But let's discuss the exception: embedded systems. Python traditional implementations are not incredibly spare users of memory. In an embedded system, you need to have that. However, if not Python itself, some dialect can address that problem.

Specifically, the dialect of Python that addresses the embedded language device programming Internet of things world is known as MicroPython. The BBC, I hear, is distributing, or has distributed, something like a million devices running MicroPython to schoolchildren.

Driscoll: So is this Python?

Martelli: It's not full Python, because it has to put some constraints on memory use.

You cannot just dynamically allocate memory in a two-dollar device. It's got to have 64K, or a fixed amount of memory. But you can still, with some limitations about this dynamic allocation, do a lot of your programming.

There are some implementation peculiarities that in the past have blocked Python from some applications, but they're being attacked. I know that Larry Hastings is slaving away at removing the Global Interpreter Lock (GIL). Despite what people think, the GIL is irrelevant to 90% of applications, but it is a killer for the 10% which desperately need to use the increasing number of cores that chip manufacturers stuff in.

If you have an algorithm optimized to use all of the 32 or 64 cores, then removing the GIL will make a huge difference for that tiny niche. Gradually, the limitations will go away.

> **Alex Martelli: 'At the heart of operating systems, I do not believe we'll see much more Python than we do today.'**

At the heart of operating systems, I do not believe we'll see much more Python than we do today. Python could be there where dynamic allocation is okay, but that's a small part of a kernel. Maybe some device drivers that are not time-critical can do that. But mostly, I see Python as running in user space, not in kernel space.

Driscoll: Why is that?

Martelli: The kernels will need lower-level languages, and incidentally they are desperately starting to need better ones than C, which is why I'm looking into Rust.

I would really like to see an experimental and simple OS kernel written in Rust. Anyway, it certainly has the potential for it. Python doesn't really, because of memory allocation. Also, the MicroPython trick doesn't really work all that well, because you do need some dynamism. Controlling paging is really hard there. But apart from that super hard, super core level, I do not see any limit. I can't even say the sky's the limit because gravitational waves are very much in the sky, yet we conquered those.

> **Alex Martelli: 'I can't even say the sky's the limit because gravitational waves are very much in the sky, yet we conquered those.'**

The only thing I can think of is that we still have a way to go with mobile development with Python. I hear good things, but I have no personal experience with Kivy.

It's a real pity, because I remember Guido chatting with Andy Rubin when they were both at Google, and trying to convince Andy that beyond Java, Android needed an application-level programming language that was much easier to use. Andy stuck to his idea that adding more languages makes things harder for programmers. It's not true! Unfortunately, Andy was the one in charge of the project, so Guido couldn't make any headway. But it would be a different world if I'd managed to be more convincing somehow.

Driscoll: So what's it like to work at Google?

Martelli: I have found it all I hoped for when I interviewed there 13 years ago and possibly more!

Of course, for me, it has been the culmination of a long and very varied career. So my expectations were not the shiny-eyed ones of somebody fresh out of some college. They were tempered by having observed what happens in reality in firms operating in the marketplace. Nevertheless, it got easily surpassed and I'm not even sure it's so much about the firm, because it's about the people. Well okay, a firm is made up of its people. The people being absolutely incredible is what makes the place absolutely incredible.

In the end, the secret is to have a bunch of awesome people! Now that was probably easier when Google had 70 employees, rather than 70,000. I mean, I'm not saying it's easy to find 70 great people, but it's certainly harder to find 70,000! It doesn't have to be 100% I guess, but it should be close to 100% awesome people.

> **Alex Martelli: 'In the end, the secret is to have a bunch of awesome people!'**

By awesome people, I don't necessarily mean just brilliant. I'm sure it's much easier to find brilliant people than to find the right kind of people, who care for the end-users, their colleagues and their partners on a human level. I mean it's important being bright and everything, but a bright asshole can do more damage than a dim one, right? So what you want first is the people who care: people who are emotionally invested in the success of their teams, their suppliers, and their users.

Driscoll: Is there a magic to finding that?

Martelli: I don't think so! You can read all the books published out there, but I just don't think so! Because faking being so caring and things in an interview is much easier than actually being so year after year. So you could get it wrong.

> **Alex Martelli: 'Anything you do can potentially be amplified and can have an impact that's completely disproportionate.'**

On a technical level, the whole size of the company poses problems and challenges of course. But it's also where you can get the greatest satisfaction from work. Anything you do can potentially be amplified and can have an impact that's completely disproportionate.

Just to give you one example: I did say I am active on Stack Overflow. Part of that is the job I do today, which is tech support for Google Cloud Platform, and this in good part happens through Stack Overflow. Well, Stack Overflow itself tells me I have helped more than 50 million people. Now, I don't know how they guess, but I certainly hope it's true! I would have met my goal of paying back all of the help that I was given by others and then some.

I know I haven't reached anywhere like that order of magnitude with my books. If I'm lucky, my books may have helped, including multiple readers per copy, a million people. It just doesn't get to 50 million. That's what being at Google can mean.

Driscoll: Are there any downsides to this?

Martelli: Of course, beware! A mistake gets amplified just as much! A little oops, and you send some system down for an hour. Whoops! Now you have inconvenienced at the very least 50 million people. But I like playing on this larger-than-life scenario.

> **Alex Martelli: 'Teaching something, so helping out somebody who's having a problem, can be the best way to learn about that issue yourself.'**

Teaching something, so helping out somebody who's having a problem, can be the best way to learn about that issue yourself. You're looking at it from the outside in a sense, but then getting in, getting involved, and getting engaged. You can exit from the experience with a much better understanding of that subject.

Driscoll: How does Google use Python?

Martelli: Okay, so it's a long story, but let's start before Google existed. A book I strongly recommend is *In the Plex* by Steven Levy. He was given unprecedented access to Google and Googlers to write this book.

One thing I learned from that book is that, well before Google had a name, Larry Page in his Stanford University dormitory was trying to write a spider to get a copy of the web onto local machines, to process and experiment with. He wanted to use this new language, Java 1.0 beta, but the whole thing kept crashing. So Larry turned to his dormitory roommate asking, "Hey, can you help me here? I just can't get this program to run!"

The roommate took a look and then said, "Well, of course not! It's that junk Java thing! Come on! Let's use a real programming language!"

Larry got Python and 100 lines of Python later, the first spider was born, and a copy of the web was finding its way to the computer in this dormitory room. So in a sense, without Python to help write the very first spider, Google might never have been born!

> **Alex Martelli: 'Without Python to help write the very first spider, Google might never have been born!'**

The spider is such a crucial program that it must have been rewritten a million times, and I'm pretty sure right now it's the most optimized bit of C++ you can imagine. I haven't looked at it for years, but the creation history is still valid. The next big role for Python and Google was as a unifying language for all of the deep infrastructure tasks.

Driscoll: What was your role at that time?

Martelli: That's where I came in as an uber tech leader for infrastructure. Instead of Bash, Perl, and other powerful, but harder to read languages, everything had to be recast into Python.

That was my first job and essentially my team and I went around working with reliability engineers, system administrators, and so on, who had written very useful utilities in Bash or Perl. We understood exactly what was going on, rewrote them, and productionized them in Python. It was a hundred times more readable.

The next big hit was Google's attempt to address the market for streaming videos. If you've ever heard of a project called Google Video, that was where Google would hold all the videos, show them to you, and let you search for them. It had, for the time, very substantial investment behind it: hundreds of brilliant engineers and hardware resources like there was no tomorrow.

Google Video kept losing the feature battle to this tiny start-up a few miles away. Each time this little start-up unveiled a new successful feature that customers liked a lot, our engineers would scramble to put up something similar and take a month or two. Each time we launched something new and innovative, that little start-up had it done in a week!

Driscoll: Did you find out how the start-up was moving so quickly?

Martelli: Eventually, we bought that little start-up and we found out how 20 developers ran circles around our hundreds of great developers. The solution was very simple! Those 20 guys were using Python. We were using C++. So, that was YouTube and still is.

> **lex Martelli: 'We found out how 20 developers ran circles around our hundreds of great developers. The solution was very simple! Those 20 guys were using Python.'**

YouTube, of course, took many years to fully develop and especially to monetize, because the amount of resources it was using was huge! It grew in popularity gradually and it's a great success story for Python.

Other areas of user-facing code vary. Sometimes Python is at the forefront, for example Google App Engine (our first foray into cloud, and still a very innovative product to this day) had Python as the first supported language. For years Python was the only language you could use there. Then Java was added and then others. But Python remains the most popular language used by customers on App Engine.

There is other stuff in the Google Cloud Platform where we have to, for technical reasons, limit the languages that our customers can use to program. Python is typically always number one or number two. TensorFlow may be another great example there. I mentioned it earlier, but the point is that TensorFlow is the most popular GitHub downloading there has been for a long time.

The existence of App Engine has biased a lot of internal tools. The ones that could be deployed on an internal-facing version of App Engine could use Python by preference, and the setup is sufficiently general that you can do almost everything that way. So in practice, from the day I joined Google 12 and a half years ago, I've had to do a little C++, especially when I was fixing existing systems. But it's been essentially all Python all the way for me.

Driscoll: Is there anything else that you'd like to discuss?

Martelli: I'd like to discuss the role of Python in education. At one point, maybe over 10 years ago, there was even a funded project that Guido worked on to put Python in a core role for education. It was never really finished. Some great things came out of it, but the taking over of education just didn't happen.

Nowadays, Python is the number one programming language used in college introductory courses. It overtook Java and others quite a while ago. But in high school, that's not the case. It seems that with the importance of computers growing, just a basic level of understanding is appropriate for most high school students. They're using an unholy mix of languages.

So what could we do to make Python more attractive for this role? What I'm thinking is that having it online and able to be run through a browser would be good. There are several sites that offer such features, but not in scalable and uniform ways.

I think that the Python Software Foundation (PSF) could put an effort behind it. Why is that? Well, because Chromebooks are the leading machines in education today. By far, more Chromebooks are selling to schools than all other kinds of devices put together. Why? They're cheap, they're powerful enough, they're secure and they're very easy to control from the administrator's viewpoint.

> **Alex Martelli: 'I think Python does not need changes, but infrastructure work to make a highly available site for schools.'**

Whatever you can do on a Chromebook, meaning essentially on a good browser on the web, is much easier to get into the curriculum than something you have to install on whatever operating system.

I think Python does not need changes, but infrastructure work to make a highly available site for schools with the kind of features schools need, such as administrator control. This would make a real difference to the lives of millions of schoolchildren. So that's my plea for anybody who's wondering what cool project they could start next with Python.

Driscoll: Thank you, Alex Martelli.

8

MARC-ANDRÉ LEMBURG

Marc-André Lemburg is a German software developer and entrepreneur. He is the CEO and founder of eGenix, which provides Python training and consulting services. Marc-André is a core developer for Python and the creator of a set of popular Python extensions. He is a founding member of the Python Software Foundation (PSF) and has served as a director twice. Marc-André is the co-founder of the Python Meeting Düsseldorf and the chair of the EuroPython Society (EPS). He regularly gives talks at Python conferences around the world.

Discussion themes: mx packages, the PSF, v2.7/v3.x.
Catch up with Marc-André Lemburg here: @malemburg

Mike Driscoll: So why did you become a programmer?

Marc-André Lemburg: My father worked at IBM, so I was exposed to programming computers quite early.

I loved technology and making things work, but at the time (late in the 1970s), computers were still pretty much out of reach for kids of my age. I played around with "programs" which were written down on a piece of paper and "run" by imagining how a real computer would probably execute them.

I learned programming aged 11, after my dad purchased a Sinclair ZX81. First, I learned BASIC and then later Z80 assembler, since the ZX81 was a rather slow machine. Assembler was particularly fun. I had to write the programs by literally putting together the opcodes bit by bit, based on a Z80 manual. I then converted the opcodes to hex and entered them into a hex editor for the ZX81 by hand, in order to run the routines.

> **Marc-André Lemburg: 'I learned to appreciate performance, as well as pay attention to details.'**

The effort was worth it, since the routines ran much faster than the ZX81 BASIC. I learned to appreciate performance, as well as pay attention to details. A bug in the assembler code usually meant having to restart the ZX81, after running the program and having to reload everything all over again. Given the cassette drive interface, this took quite a while.

About two years later, my dad bought the first IBM PC1 and I started to learn MS BASIC, Turbo Pascal, and Turbo C. In school, I continued to work a lot with computers and during university I founded my first company.

Driscoll: So how did you come across Python?

Lemburg: I first found out about Python when looking through an OS/2 Freeware CD called Hobbes in 1994. Python was listed as one of the programming languages and included in version 1.1.

I read Guido van Rossum's tutorial in an afternoon and was immediately convinced that I had found what I had always been looking for. Python is a language which has all of the important data structures, implemented in a way that is easy to use, with a clear syntax and no need for explicit memory management or parentheses to define blocks.

At the time, I was mostly writing C code, so I had to deal with all of the difficulties of a system language on a regular basis. Problems included memory allocation, pointer arithmetic, overflows, segfaults, long sessions in debuggers, and the slow edit-compile-run-debug cycle.

> **Marc-André Lemburg: 'Python had everything that made me happy.'**

Python had everything that made me happy: an interpreter for interactive experiments, good documentation, a fairly complete standard library and a really nice C API, with everything needed to interface Python to existing C code. This included a detail which I found particularly interesting: the interpreter was using the data structures it provided for the language to also implement its own internals.

Driscoll: Could you explain how you became an entrepreneur and founded your own company?

Lemburg: I started working in IT at the age of 17. In 1993, while at university, I formed my first company called IKDS and worked as a freelancer for local companies that wanted to enter the then new market of online business.

After finishing university in 1997, I used my experience from building several website engines, to start working on a new web application server. My aim was to build a system that would make it easy and efficient to develop online web systems. The system would leverage object-oriented technology, relational databases, and the simplicity and elegance of Python.

After three years of hard work, I had finished the first release, with everything that was needed for a commercial enterprise product. I then started a limited company to market the product early in 2000. The development of the application server resulted in me entering the world of open source.

> **Marc-André Lemburg: 'The development of the application server resulted in me entering the world of open source.'**

Since I did not have enough resources available to thoroughly test the software that I was writing, I decided to make the basic modules used in the application server open source. This is how the popular mx Extensions came to be. Commercially, the application server was not a success. I found that the market simply didn't yet understand the benefits of such a product.

I then focused more on consulting and running projects for other companies. One of the more interesting projects was a financial trading system that was completely written in Python. Similar projects are keeping me fairly busy these days, so I unfortunately don't have much time to contribute to CPython development anymore.

Driscoll: Can you explain a little more about the mx Extensions that your company distributes and maintains?

Lemburg: I started working on the mx Extensions while developing the web application server in 1997. At the time, I found that Python was lacking a good general-purpose database module.

There was an old Windows-based ODBC interface, but it wasn't really up to the task of providing a viable and performant interface to databases across Windows and Unix platforms. I started writing mxODBC to address this need. I wanted to create a fast and portable interface for ODBC drivers, which would allow me to connect the application server to all of the popular databases.

While working on mxODBC, the lack of a good date/time handling module became apparent. mxDateTime was born to fix this and became a standard in the Python world for many years, until the Python stdlib grew its own datetime module in Python 2.3.

> **Marc-André Lemburg: 'mxDateTime was born...and became a standard in the Python world for many years.'**

mxTextTools and several of the other mx packages were the result of needing fast parsing for templating in the application server. This was later used by other people to write parsing engines, for example Biopython (parsing genome data), or drive parsers implementing user-defined grammars.

The Tagging Engine in mxTextTools works a bit like a Turing state machine, because it provides very fast parsing primitives, which can be assembled using Python tuples. Several utility functions help with using the parsing results for implementing search and replace. mxTextTools was first written for 8-bit text and binary data. A few years later, a client hired me to extend this to Unicode.

The lesser known mxStack and mxQueue played a role as fast data structures in the application server. The mxTools package is a collection of fast built-ins that I also wrote for the application server. Several of the ideas in mxTools were eventually added to core Python in some form.

Driscoll: So how did you become a Python core developer?

Lemburg: While starting to write the mx Extensions, I had a lot of contact with the Python C API and its internals. I contributed back patches to CPython and became a core developer later in 1997.

Probably more people know about my contributions to CPython in the form of the Unicode integration. In 1999, Guido contacted Fredrik Lundh and me and asked us to bring Unicode to Python. This was initiated by a grant from HP to the Python Consortium (a Python Software Foundation predecessor).

> **Marc-André Lemburg: 'Guido contacted Fredrik Lundh and me and asked us to bring Unicode to Python.'**

Fredrik worked on a new regular expression engine. I added native Unicode support to Python. I also designed and wrote the codec subsystem in Python. The initial release was in 2000, with Python 1.6/2.0. I helped to maintain this part of CPython 2.0 for more than 10 years.

Driscoll: What are some of the other contributions that you have made to Python?

Lemburg: I contributed the source code encoding system, the platform module and parts of the locale module. I was also responsible for the pybench suite for measuring enhancements to CPython and several patches and ideas to make Python run faster, or to make it more comfortable.

Driscoll: What challenges have you had as a core developer of Python?

Lemburg: In the early years, being a core developer was a lot of fun, since the processes were a lot less formal than they are today. The only real challenge was that discussions targeting Unicode often resulted in endless discussions and sometimes flame wars.

> **Marc-André Lemburg: 'Discussions targeting Unicode often resulted in endless discussions and sometimes flame wars.'**

I don't know whether this was because Unicode was at the core of working with text, or simply due to the many strong egos participating in the discussions. I took most of these discussions with a grain of salt and good humor.

Since then, we've seen several generations of core developers come and move on. Integrating the new developers was often not easy and involved lots of discussions. We had to try to explain how Python development worked and move all of the new energy in the right directions.

Driscoll: Python is one of the major languages used in AI and machine learning. Why do you think this is?

Lemburg: Python is very easy to understand for scientists who are often not trained in computer science. It removes many of the complexities that you have to deal with, when trying to drive the external libraries that you need to perform research.

After Numeric (now NumPy) started the development, the addition of IPython Notebooks (now Jupyter Notebooks), matplotlib, and many other tools to make things even more intuitive, Python has allowed scientists to mainly think about solutions to problems and not so much about the technology needed to drive these solutions.

> **Marc-André Lemburg: 'Python has allowed scientists to mainly think about solutions to problems and not so much about the technology needed to drive these solutions.'**

As in other areas, Python is an ideal integration language, which binds technologies together with ease. Python allows users to focus on the real problems, rather than spending time on implementation details. Apart from making things easier for the user, Python also shines as an ideal glue platform for the people who develop the low-level integrations with external libraries. This is mainly due to Python being very accessible via a nice and very complete C API.

Driscoll: How could Python be improved for AI and machine learning?

Lemburg: I think that Python is already one of the best choices that you have for AI and machine learning. With a vibrant community engaged in making the language even better, Python is going to have a long and great future in this area.

Mike Driscoll: Can you explain how the Python Software Foundation (PSF) was founded?

Lemburg: Before the PSF we had the Python Software Activity group (PSA), for which you had to pay a small amount each year. We also had the lesser known Python Consortium, for companies to support Python development, which paid big bucks each year.

Both groups did not really provide enough support for Python. The copyright in Python was also scattered across several different companies (see the Python license stack). Two companies that had significantly invested in Python, Zope Corporation, and ActivePython, started a project to potentially address all of these issues with a new non-profit organization.

This became the PSF and it was founded at IPC9, the commercial International Python Conference 9. We had 16 Python core developers at the time and the two companies as founding members. The core developers, including Guido, licensed their contributions to the PSF by signing contributor agreements and all subsequent releases were done in the name of the PSF.

Initially, the PSF did nothing more than work as a legal body for maintaining the copyright in Python distribution. Later, the PSF also received the trademark rights to the wordmark Python from CNRI.

In 2003, the PSF then underwrote the first PyCon US conference in Washington. This new development introduced a revenue stream for the PSF, which opened up new possibilities for helping the Python community.

> **Marc-André Lemburg: 'This new development introduced a revenue stream for the PSF, which opened up new possibilities for helping the Python community.'**

As PyCon US grew and commercial sponsors started supporting it more, the revenue also grew. This resulted in the PSF turning into a more mature organization over the years. I was on the PSF board for several years to help with these developments.

Driscoll: I know that you helped to organize the first EuroPython. Could you tell me about that?

Lemburg: In 2001, a group of European Python and Zope users and companies started a long discussion about the desire to have a Python conference in Europe.

The Python workshops and the IPC conferences were all in the US. There wasn't much going on for Python in Europe at the time. I was one of the participants in the discussions and they did not seem to want to end. Closer to the event, I then joined the executive committee to actually make the EuroPython conference happen. That's how EuroPython 2002 came to be.

> **Marc-André Lemburg: 'There wasn't much going on for Python in Europe at the time.'**

The whole event was run by volunteers, unlike the commercial Python conferences in the US at the time. We were on a very small budget. As such, EuroPython also predates PyCon US, which was the first conference that was run by volunteers in the US.

EuroPython 2002 was held in Charleroi. It was a lot of fun to be able to run a first major European Python conference. EuroPython was also quite successful, with even Guido attending. Nowadays, there are lots of national Python events happening each year, so while EuroPython doesn't want to compete with other national Python events, it's definitely operating in that space.

Driscoll: How has EuroPython changed over the years?

Lemburg: Since the early days, EuroPython has grown a lot and it passed the 1000 attendee mark in 2014. The conference is still run by volunteers, but it's no longer an operation which can be run on the side.

The EuroPython Society, which organizes EuroPython, has a lot of work to do each year to put on the conference. I'm the chair of the organization at the moment and have been on the board for several years. Each year, we're growing the event into a more professional setup. Still, it's a challenge staying on top of everything that needs to be done to put on a conference. The board members typically have to work between 200 and 400 hours each to make an event happen.

Driscoll: What are you most excited about in Python today?

Lemburg: I'm most excited about the native async I/O support. With the addition of new keywords, this has finally become usable in Python and will go a long way in helping to use the full CPU power that's available on today's machines.

> **Marc-André Lemburg: 'I'm most excited about the native async I/O support.'**

As an aside, I find the Python type annotations to be the least exciting development in today's Python. They take away a lot of the elegance of Python programs. Even though type annotations are optional, many companies will enforce their use via corporate policy. This will eventually result in more and more Python being written using these annotations and will make Python look a lot like any other modern statically typed scripting language.

Driscoll: What do you think about Python 2.7? Should everyone be moving over to the latest version?

Lemburg: Yes, they should, but you have to consider the amount of work which has to go into a port from Python 2.7 to 3.x. Many companies have huge code bases written for Python 2.x, including my own company eGenix. Commercially, it doesn't always make sense to port to Python 3.x, so the divide between the two worlds will continue to exist well beyond 2020.

> **Marc-André Lemburg: 'Commercially, it doesn't always make sense to port to Python 3.x, so the divide between the two worlds will continue to exist well beyond 2020.'**

Python 2.7 does have its advantages because it became the LTS version of Python. Corporate users generally like these long-term support versions, since they reduce porting efforts from one version to the next.

I believe that Python will have to come up with an LTS 3.x version as well, to be able to sustain success in the corporate world. Once we settle on such a version, this will also make a more viable case for a Python 2.7 port, since the investment will then be secured for a good number of years.

Driscoll: What changes would you like to see in future Python releases?

Lemburg: Python will need to make it easier to use the full number of cores and CPUs that you have in today's machines. Async I/O has helped by making better use of a single core, but it's not the answer to multi-core deployments.

Removing the Global Interpreter Lock (GIL) and replacing it with more fine-grained locking mechanisms would be one approach, but it's going to be a long and rocky path to such a world. We should be careful not to underestimate the complexities and possible breakage to the many C extensions. Alienating these would set back Python a lot, since they are essential drivers of Python's success. As a result, we would have to provide a smooth upgrade path for the existing extensions, perhaps by keeping the GIL in place while they are in control.

In my opinion, we should also investigate other approaches, such as making inter-process communication more efficient and user friendly, perhaps even by adding new keywords to automatically run code in parallel.

Driscoll: Thank you, Marc-André Lemburg.

9

Barry Warsaw

Barry Warsaw is an American software engineer and a member of the Python Foundation team at LinkedIn. Barry worked for Canonical for 10 years, becoming an Ubuntu and Debian developer with responsibility for the Python ecosystem on those operating systems. He was the project leader of GNU Mailman, a popular open source mailing list manager written in Python. Barry's former roles include lead maintainer for Jython, Python release manager and member of PythonLabs. Today he is a core developer, the author of several successful Python Enhancement Proposals, and the maintainer of numerous Python libraries.

Discussion themes: PythonLabs, Python's future, v2.7/v3.x.

Catch up with Barry Warsaw here: @pumpichank

Mike Driscoll: How did you end up becoming a programmer?

Barry Warsaw: I started programming when I was pretty young. Computers then were actually Teletype machines, that were connected to mainframes in the school and the main school district. So I got on the Teletypes.

I learned BASIC, which was really fun. I remember in the summer of that year, some of the kids in another school used those same Teletypes to break into the mainframes in the Board of Education. So the next year they pulled them all out of the schools and gave us 6502-based PCs. The teachers didn't know how to use them at all, so I taught the teachers.

The guidance counselors took notice of what I was doing. They hooked me up with summer internships at what was then called the National Bureau of Standards (NBS), a federal research facility in Gaithersburg, Maryland. The NBS is where I learned to love sharing programs and collaborating with other people.

Driscoll: So did you work with NBS all through high school?

Warsaw: Yes, I interned with NBS through high school and through college. Then I got a full-time job at what is now called the National Institute of Standards and Technology (NIST) and I worked there until 1990.

My internships and then full-time job at NIST were eye-opening, because I didn't actually know what the real industry was like, or what it was like to be a professional programmer.

> **Barry Warsaw: 'I didn't actually know what the real industry was like, or what it was like to be a professional programmer.'**

I worked with the robotics team at the time and although I wasn't doing much robotics, I did find myself working on the graphical user interfaces for industrial robots for factory automation. That work was just amazing. From there I got into system administration. A few years into that we got a lot of Sun-3s, so we learned SunOS, Unix, C programming, Emacs, and all kinds of things like that.

I was a computer science undergraduate and it was fine, but I really learned the trade by doing real programming at NIST. I've noticed that college classes don't exactly prepare you for what you actually end up doing.

> **Barry Warsaw: 'I really learned the trade by doing real programming at NIST.'**

For example, I was talking to some current interns and they said that in college, at least as undergraduates, you don't even learn version control systems, such as using Git. That is just amazing to me. I can't believe how divorced from the reality of working programmers the college environment is. It is very shocking when you get out of college and it's completely different to what you were taught.

Driscoll: Do you think that Python offers a pathway to real programming, as you call it, for new programmers?

Warsaw: Yes, when I'm talking to kids today that use Python, these kids have often somehow hooked up with a project on GitHub. Sometimes they've even come to a Python conference and stayed for the sprints.

Kids learn so much more about modern software engineering best practices that way. You can really see it. They come in and they understand how to do pull requests and how to file good bugs. I tell all the young kids that I talk with to find a GitHub, GitLab, or even Bitbucket project that interests them and start getting involved.

Python, of course, is an amazing community for that. It's so welcoming to a diverse group of people. In the Python community we're friendly, we accept anybody, and we guide and mentor them. So I also tell students who really want to learn how to do it right to come to the Python community and get engaged, because they are going to learn so much by doing that.

Driscoll: How did you end up getting into Python yourself?

Warsaw: In 1994, I met Roger Masse. His girlfriend (and current wife) and my wife were very friendly, so we'd all get together for dinner. Rog and I really connected on a geek level.

Rog had just started a job at CNRI, which is the Corporation for National Research Initiatives in Virginia (CNRI was started by Bob Kahn and Vint Cerf, who are two of the fathers of TCP/IP.) So in the late summer of 1994, I started working for CNRI too.

I was working on a project called knowbots. These were little software agents that would bundle themselves up and move to a different host. The knowbots would do some work over at another host and then move around the internet to find information for you. Rog and I started working on that project in Objective-C on NeXT machines.

A little later, some friends who were still at NIST told me about a Dutch guy who was coming to give a little workshop on this language that he had invented. They asked whether I'd be interested, so we did a little bit of research. Of course, it was Guido van Rossum, and the language was Python, so we said, "Sure, we'd love to come."

> **Barry Warsaw: 'A Dutch guy...was coming to give a little workshop on this language that he had invented. They asked whether I'd be interested, so we did a little bit of research. Of course, it was Guido van Rossum, and the language was Python.'**

We wanted to talk to Guido about some of his ideas, because we thought that Python could be really cool for this Objective-C project. We thought we could script Objective-C in Python.

The workshop was in November of 1994. There were only 20 of us and we just fell in love with Python and Guido. He was just so open and cool and the workshop was really fantastic. I think both Guido and I were fans of Emacs, so we talked about how docstrings in Python could work a little bit syntactically, or at least syntactically like docstrings in Emacs Lisp.

After the workshop, we went back to CNRI and were just gushing about how we thought Python was going to work really well. One of our colleagues said, "Hey, why don't we try to hire Guido?" We didn't know if he wanted to come to the United States, or would be interested in working on this Objective-C Python thing, or the knowbot project. But he was, so in April of 1995 Guido started at CNRI.

We moved a lot of the infrastructure from the Netherlands to Virginia. I think at the time it was a CVS repository. So we pulled the CVS repository over, did a lot of the system administration stuff for Python, and of course got into developing Python as well.

> **Barry Warsaw: 'Python 1.2 was the first version that we released out of CNRI. So it was in some ways very much today's Python.'**

I knew C pretty well at the time, so we did a lot of work on the C internals of Python and then also the Python standard library. I think Python 1.2 was the first version that we released out of CNRI. So it was in some ways very much today's Python. Even Python 3 has the same feel to it that Python did way back then. Although there are so many amazing new features, that I don't know whether you would recognize it.

I seem to remember that although Python had classes, it didn't even have keyword arguments. We were doing a lot of things with Tcl/Tk graphically. The signatures of functions got ridiculous, because even though most of the arguments were None, you had to pass them all in. So that was the motivation for doing keyword arguments. Anyway, CNRI was great and working with Guido on Python was fantastic. We did that until Guido moved on.

Driscoll: Steve Holden said that you were part of PythonLabs. Were you one of the founders?

Warsaw: Yes, in 2000 a bunch of us left CNRI to seek our fortunes with Python. It was the five of us: Tim Peters, Jeremy Hilton, Fred Drake, myself, and Guido. Roger stayed at CNRI. That group was what we called PythonLabs, but it was more of an inside joke. I mean, it wasn't really an official thing.

> **Barry Warsaw: 'In 2000 a bunch of us left CNRI to seek our fortunes with Python.'**

We joined BeOpen, but that lasted for a few months and then went away. Then we all moved over to Zope Corporation. We just felt like we had a little club made up of the five of us who had come from CNRI and Tim Peters, of course. So that's really what PythonLabs was. I even made a joke at one time on the mailing list and asked Tim whether PythonLabs still exists. If you go to pythonlab.com, you'll find the very humorous response from Tim to my question.

Driscoll: Did you guys have specific roles in PythonLabs?

Warsaw: Not really, although Guido really led the work that we did on Python and the work that we did with Python.

I can't remember many of the details about what we did in the beginning, even with Zope Corporation. Of course, we all had tasks to do within Zope Corporation, but then we would get together and work on Python itself.

> **Barry Warsaw: 'We worked on what we found interesting, which was internals, new features, bug fixes or infrastructure.'**

We worked on what we found interesting, which was internals, new features, bug fixes, or infrastructure. All of that stuff really needed to be done back then, because the Python community was so much smaller than it is now.

Driscoll: So were there any goals at that time for the Python language that you guys were shooting for?

Warsaw: You know, it's hard for me to remember the exact timeline, but I'm sure someone could do the archaeology and figure out what the features were. I do remember the big pushes.

One of the earliest things that I did at CNRI was work with Roger on what was called the grand renaming. The Python C source code back at that time didn't have the nice clean namespaces that the C API has now. They were all just named in a global namespace.

The problem with that was that people were trying to embed Python, but it wasn't going to work because those names were colliding with their own symbols. So we did the grand renaming, where we went through the entire internal C API and cleaned it up, so that you could embed Python in other C applications. So I remember that was one of the very first things that I did.

There was also a lot of work on new-style classes at the time, which of course in Python 3 is the only kind of class. There were a lot of discussions about how the type system would work in the new-style class infrastructure.

The other thing that I remember from the original workshop was that there was this guy named Don Beaudry. He was doing some crazy metaclass hacks. Of course, Jim Fulton was very interested in doing metaclass stuff as well. Jim was the CTO of Zope Corporation.

> **Barry Warsaw: 'By Python 2.2, we really wanted to do metaclasses right and fix some of the problems with the semantics of classic classes.'**

I remember not really understanding much about metaclasses at the original Python workshop. It went over my head at the time. However, by Python 2.2, we really wanted to do metaclasses right and fix some of the problems with the semantics of classic classes.

I remember a lot of discussions about how the new-style class stuff could work so that you could inherit from a type and define new types, as well as new instances. There were just so many features, but we all pitched in on the things that were interesting to us.

Driscoll: I seem to recall that you worked on the original email library in Python. Do you remember how that came about?

Warsaw: Yeah, so one of the things that we did early on was to move the Python mailing list to CNRI. It was still being run at CWI, which was the Dutch institute where Guido worked before he came to the US.

The Python mailing list was running on Majordomo, which was the most popular mailing list software at the time, and was written all in Perl. When we moved it over, there were a lot of things that we wanted to improve. By the way, Ken Manheimer actually crops up here because he was very instrumental in the early days of Mailman.

So we pulled the Majordomo installation over to CNRI, but it was really inconvenient making the changes to it that we wanted to make, because we didn't enjoy developing in Perl. We're Pythonistas, right?

> **Barry Warsaw: 'We didn't enjoy developing in Perl. We're Pythonistas, right?'**

We had a friend by the name of John Viega, who was going to the University of Virginia. John was friends with the guys in the Dave Matthews Band before they were big. So John wanted to write a little mailing list manager in Python, that he could use to connect the fans with the band and send out announcements. He wrote the mailing list manager, and we caught wind of it.

We thought that maybe we could work on this thing for Python mailing lists, because it would be better to have a Python-based mailing list manager. So we got a copy of the mailing list manager, but John lost the disc and the original copy of what eventually became Mailman. Fortunately, Ken had a copy that he resurrected and we were able to start working on it to support the mailing list for the Python community.

We decided that we would call the mailing list manager Mailman. We then put it into the GNU Project and put the GPL on it. I personally got really involved with Mailman. It was interesting and I really loved the aspect of allowing people to communicate.

> **Barry Warsaw: 'I really loved the aspect of allowing people to communicate.'**

The other really cool thing about the early Mailman software was that it had a web interface, which was something that Majordomo didn't have at the time. That was one of the defining factors, in my opinion, of Mailman.

One of the things that I realized was that there was no good RFC compliant email-parsing software. There really wasn't. There was the rfc822 module in the standard library, but it wasn't very advanced and new email standards were coming out for the format of email messages.

It became apparent that rfc822 wasn't going to cut it. So I worked on an offshoot called mimelib, that added support for MIME constructs: composing messages, having different MIME types and images. We had defined a model that described an email message, especially on MIME messages.

We wanted it to be possible to programmatically build up a tree of email messages. We had a parser so that you could feed it a bunch of Python 2 byte strings. You had this parser and it would give you a tree that represented the email message. Then you could manipulate that and pass that tree to a generator. The generator would flatten the tree back into the byte representation of an email message, along with the MIME boundaries and things like that.

We tried to be RFC compliant as best as we could. I think we were pretty successful, but they're very complicated standards. I think even now we're learning the deficiencies and the bugs in it. In any case, mimelib was a thing and I released mimelib as a separate third-party package. Then I started using mimelib in Mailman. It was a real benefit to have this third-party package that we could develop separately from Mailman and just pull in as a dependency.

I don't remember exactly when it happened, but there was a Python release when we felt that mimelib was pretty stable and the API was pretty good. So we pulled mimelib into the standard library and renamed it as the email package, which is a better name for it anyway, because there's a lot more to it than just MIME.

> **Barry Warsaw: 'We pulled mimelib into the standard library and renamed it as the email package.'**

So that's the history of the email package. It came from mimelib, which came from the work in Mailman, on top of the rfc822 module in the old Python standard library. I was actually joking with the guys that we should have called the panel session at PyCon Grandpa's Python Time! We've all been around Python for so long. We should say, "Kids! Come on up and sit around the fire. Grandpa will tell you stories about Python in the old days."

Driscoll: So we talked about Mailman. Have you learned any lessons that you would like to share from being the lead for that project?

Warsaw: I'm not sure that I'm really the best project leader! I have so many interests and find it difficult to spend the right amount of time with a project.

I am fortunate to have core developers in the Mailman project who are fantastic developers, really amazing people and super friendly. The highlight of my PyCon is to get together with the core developers to hang out socially, work on the technology, and keep it current.

> **Barry Warsaw: 'The highlight of my PyCon is to get together with the core developers to hang out socially, work on the technology, and keep it current.'**

Mailman's been around for forever now and it's still a viable project. I do think that you have to really open up, trust your core developers, and be willing to hand over parts of a project. Great web designers really understand the technology and can design a great interface that looks good and is fun to use. That's great for me because then I can concentrate on the bits that really interest and fire me up.

We've had some Google Summer of Code projects and one of our core developers came from there. He's just done an amazing amount of work on our Docker images and some of the glue layers. It's just really great to be able to have developers that you really like to work with, that you know are just really smart and friendly.

You need to have developers that will put forth that kind of community aspect that I like with Python. The Python community is welcoming and friendly, with a focus on mentoring people as they come in. So I think another lesson is to be open with what you do and give your time and your expertise, because it will come back tenfold.

> **Barry Warsaw: 'I think another lesson is to be open with what you do and give your time and your expertise.'**

Driscoll: Have you had any challenges with the Mailman project that you didn't expect to have?

Warsaw: Oh yeah. I don't get this too much these days but because Mailman is free and we give it away, we don't really even know all of the people who use it.

We don't control Mailman in any way and we don't tell people what they can and cannot do with it. Most people use it for very good things, such as for their biking club, or certainly in a lot of tech discussion lists. But some people do use Mailman for nefarious purposes, like spamming people. One of the challenges is that we get contacted when people have been spammed by unscrupulous developers and we get a lot of threatening emails at times, which is very disheartening.

One of the things that I've learned is that people reach out to you in those cases when they are frustrated. They're going through pain because they're getting spammed by somebody. They don't know who is spamming them and they're not getting any relief from that person, so they search around.

Now, we put very prominent notices that we do not condone spam and we do not approve of using Mailman for any kind of illegal purposes. We encourage people to use Mailman for opt-in, so that you know that you're signing up for something. But we can't really control it.

> **Barry Warsaw: 'One of the things that I have found helpful is to let people know that there is a human on the other side of Mailman.'**

We don't have any kind of administrative access, but people reach out to us in moments of frustration. One of the things that I have found helpful is to let people know that there is a human on the other side of Mailman. Sometimes we'll do a little bit of research to see if we can find a contact, or find their hosting provider. Even the most frustrated person is normally very appreciative of that.

So that was really challenging back in the early days. People would send very nasty emails to my personal email address and that gets really frustrating. There are all kinds of people out there on the internet, right?

Driscoll: So when we spoke for the PyDev of the Week series, you mentioned that you worked at Canonical. What was it like to work at a Linux distribution company?

Warsaw: Well, it was really awesome. I stopped working there in April, but I'd been there for ten years. I really enjoyed it and it was a great position to be in, because I felt that I could really help the Python community for Ubuntu and Debian.

Working at Canonical was a great nexus for helping people who were consumers of a Linux distro, like Ubuntu or Debian, and users of Python on those platforms. I'm a core developer for Python, so when a problem would occur, I was able to see whether the fix needed to go in Debian or Ubuntu and ask whether it needed to go in upstream Python or go in some library.

> **Barry Warsaw: 'I'm a core developer for Python, so when a problem would occur, I was able to see whether the fix needed to go in Debian or Ubuntu and ask whether it needed to go in upstream Python or go in some library.'**

So I really had the opportunity to work very closely with a wide range of Python projects. I was also able to interact with Python itself and work on areas of Python that I thought needed to be improved for distribution on the Linux distro. So it was really fun. It was a great experience and I'm really glad that I had the opportunity to do it.

Driscoll: What exactly did you do in your role at Canonical? Could you explain that?

Warsaw: Yes, so I was a member of the Foundations team, which was a small team that worked on this sort of plumbing layer of a Linux distro.

So imagine, at the bottommost part you have a kernel, right? We didn't do any kernel work because we had a separate kernel team. But above that you had things like the boot process, compilers, toolchains, and package building the archive health. So as things landed in the archive, you wanted to make sure that it was stable and robust. It's all this sort of random mix of things above the kernel, but below the desktop.

One of the things that the Foundation team was responsible for was language interpreters. Python is fairly popular for writing scripts that the operating system itself and the build processes use, so it is a pretty important language for Ubuntu and many Linux distributions.

> **Barry Warsaw: 'One of the things that I was responsible for was the general health of the Python ecosystem on Ubuntu.'**

One of the things that I was responsible for was the general health of the Python ecosystem on Ubuntu. That included working on transitions, like trying to move everybody to Python 3. Then as new versions of Python would come out, while I didn't directly do the interpreter, I did work on all the packages that were involved.

There are a lot of steps that you have to go through in order to make Python 3.5 the default version on Ubuntu. It's a long process. A lot of packages won't build, or they have bugs in the new version of Python, so you have to fix those, prioritize and stuff like that. So one of the main things that I did on Ubuntu was really work on the Python ecosystem.

Again, I was looking at the tools and seeing what pain points Ubuntu developers were having with the Python tools. I was trying to figure out how to improve them and where to improve them. For example, if there was some friction with using pip and setuptools on Ubuntu, then the fixes might have to go into pip and setuptools. It was my responsibility to be aware of where people were having pains using Ubuntu.

> **Barry Warsaw: 'I was looking at the tools and seeing what pain points Ubuntu developers were having with the Python tools. I was trying to figure out how to improve them and where to improve them.'**

In addition, I did a lot of consulting with people who were using Python on Ubuntu. If people had Python questions, I would work with them, answer their questions, and do code reviews.

I also worked with a lot of people in the community. If community people on Ubuntu had questions about how Python worked, or had problems, I was one of the people they could talk to and work with. A lot of it is community-driven, but I think if you really want to make a distribution a success, then you have to put resources into it. Every Linux distribution puts resources into its communities, because otherwise it's just going to fall apart.

> **Barry Warsaw: 'A lot of it is community-driven, but I think if you really want to make a distribution a success, then you have to put resources into it.'**

Driscoll: Let's move on to a slightly different topic. What do you think makes Python such a good language for AI and machine learning right now?

Warsaw: Python is a fantastic glue language. It's also very easy to learn and use, both for expert programmers and for researchers, for whom programming is not their primary vocation.

I think both of these aspects make Python a great language for domains like machine learning. The language is very malleable as you experiment, but robust as you build bigger systems. I think this is also a contributing factor to why we see Python becoming so popular in the data sciences. These are often technologies where programming isn't the central occupation, but kind of secondary to the core research being conducted.

Driscoll: What could we do to make Python an even better language for AI and machine learning?

Warsaw: I'm not sure that much needs to change with Python, but it's possible that the Python ecosystem could be improved to give more visibility to AI/machine learning libraries, and make it easier to integrate such libraries with other Python applications, frameworks, and libraries.

Driscoll: So, just because I'm curious, what are you doing now?

Warsaw: I just started working with LinkedIn a couple of weeks ago. I really like it. I think it's a great company and they use a lot of Python. So I'm still doing Python work. I'm working on Python within LinkedIn and I love the team.

I think LinkedIn has a great mission and I am psyched about what the company is trying to do. The mission is to connect people with economic opportunities, so it's kind of funny that LinkedIn helped me to find a job and that job happened to be with LinkedIn!

LinkedIn also has a lot of other stuff that it does. I really like the focus on helping people to find the right fit for whatever they want to do in their professional career.

Driscoll: Since you have such a deep knowledge of Python, could you tell me where you see Python going as a language in the future?

Warsaw: That's a really interesting question. I think in some ways it's hard to predict where Python is going. I've been involved in Python for 23 years, and there was no way I could have predicted in 1994 what the computing world was going to look like today.

> **Barry Warsaw: 'I've been involved in Python for 23 years, and there was no way I could have predicted in 1994 what the computing world was going to look like today.'**

I look at phones, IoT (Internet of things) devices, and just the whole landscape of what computing looks like today, with the cloud and containers. It's just amazing to look around and see all of that stuff. So there's no real way to predict what Python is going to look like even five years from now, and certainly not ten or fifteen years from now.

I do think Python's future is still very bright, but I think Python, and especially CPython, which is the implementation of Python in C, has challenges. Any language that's been around for that long is going to have some challenges. Python was invented to solve problems in the 90s and the computing world is different now and is going to become different still.

> **Barry Warsaw: 'Python was invented to solve problems in the 90s and the computing world is different now and is going to become different still.'**

I think the challenges for Python include things like performance and multi-core or multi-threading applications. There are definitely people who are working on that stuff and other implementations of Python may spring up like PyPy, Jython, or IronPython.

Aside from the challenges that the various implementations have, one thing that Python has as a language, and I think this is its real strength, is that it scales along with the human scale. For example, you can have one person write up some scripts on their laptop to solve a particular problem that they have. Python's great for that.

> **Barry Warsaw: 'One thing that Python has as a language, and I think this is its real strength, is that it scales along with the human scale.'**

Python also scales to, let's say, a small open source project with maybe 10 or 15 people contributing. Python scales to hundreds of people working on a fairly large project, or thousands of people working on massive software projects.

Another amazing strength of Python as a language is that new developers can come in and learn it easily and be productive very quickly. They can pull down a completely new Python source code for a project that they've never seen before and dive in and learn it very easily and quickly. There are some challenges as Python scales on the human scale, but I feel like those are being solved by things like the type annotations, for example.

On very large Python projects, where you have a mix of junior and senior developers, it can be a lot of effort for junior developers to understand how to use an existing library or application, because they're coming from a more statically-typed language.

So a lot of organizations that are building very large Python codebases are adopting type annotations, maybe not so much to help with the performance of the applications, but to help with the onboarding of new developers. I think that's going a long way in helping Python to continue to scale on a human scale.

> **Barry Warsaw: 'I think if we address some of those technical limitations...then we're really setting Python up for another 20 years of success and growth.'**

To me, the language's scaling capacity and the welcoming nature of the Python community are the two things that make Python still compelling even after 23 years, and will continue to make Python compelling in the future. I think if we address some of those technical limitations, which are completely doable, then we're really setting Python up for another 20 years of success and growth.

Driscoll: Do you see any new features coming to Python, or is there anything else that you're excited about?

Warsaw: Yeah, another friend of mine, Eric Smith, who's also a core developer, comes up with these great features that you don't know how you ever used Python without.

One new feature in Python 3.6 is the f-strings, the format strings. I have only used f-strings in a couple of projects, because they're a Python 3.6 feature, but I love f-strings. I also love contextlib.

> **Barry Warsaw: 'I say this with every release, but Python 3.7 is truly going to be the best ever.'**

I'm also very excited about Python 3.7. I say this with every release, but Python 3.7 is truly going to be the best ever. We're going to see some great new libraries, improved support for *asyncio*, and better performance. Python development is as vibrant as ever and I believe that the improvements to our workflow (for example, the switch to Git and GitHub) has really opened up Python development to many more people.

I love that folks can experiment with crazy ideas, like the gilectomy, which even if they don't pan out, provide fodder for future development. C Python's implementation is easy to understand, navigate, and change, and this goes a long way to making it a friendly platform for experimentation and change.

All the while, we have Guido's continued stewardship and other long-time developers providing vision and coherence, so that while Python today looks very different to Python from 20+ years ago, it still feels like the same well-designed, consistent, easy to learn, yet scalable language.

Driscoll: What do you think about the long life of Python 2.7?

Warsaw: We all know that we've got to get on Python 3, so Python 2's life is limited. I made it a mission inside of Ubuntu to try to get people to get on Python 3. Similarly, within LinkedIn, I'm really psyched, because all of my projects are on Python 3 now. Python 3 is so much more compelling than Python 2.

> **Barry Warsaw: 'We all know that we've got to get on Python 3, so Python 2's life is limited.'**

You don't even realize all of the features that you have in Python 3. One of the features that I think is really awesome is the async I/O library. I'm using that in a lot of things and think it is a very compelling new feature, that started with Python 3.4. Even with Python 3.5, with the new async keywords for I/O-based applications, *asyncio* was just amazing.

There are tons of these features that once you start to use them, you just can't go back to Python 2. It feels so primitive. I love Python 3 and use it exclusively in all of my personal open source projects. I find that dropping back to Python 2.7 is often a chore, because so many of the cool things you depend on are just missing, although some libraries are available in Python 2 compatible back ports.

I firmly believe that it's well past the time to fully embrace Python 3. I wouldn't write a line of new code that doesn't support it, although there can be business reasons to continue to support existing Python 2 code.

It's almost never that difficult to convert to Python 3, although there are still a handful of dependencies that don't support it, often because those dependencies have been abandoned. It does require resources and careful planning though, but any organization that routinely addresses technical debt should have conversion to Python 3 in their plans.

That said, the long life of Python 2.7 has been great. It's provided two important benefits I think. The first is that it provided a very stable version of Python, almost a long-term support release, so folks didn't have to even think about changes in Python every 18 months (the typical length of time new versions are in development).

> **Barry Warsaw: 'Python 2.7's long life also allowed the rest of the ecosystem to catch up with Python 3.'**

Python 2.7's long life also allowed the rest of the ecosystem to catch up with Python 3. So the folks who were very motivated to support it could sand down the sharp edges and make it much easier for others to follow. I think we now have very good tools, experience, and expertise in how to switch to Python 3 with the greatest chance of success.

I think we reached the tipping point somewhere around the Python 3.5 release. Regardless of what the numbers say, we're well past the point where there's any debate about choosing Python 3, especially for new code. Python 2.7 will end its life in mid-2020 and that's about right, although not soon enough for me! At some point, it's just more fun to develop in and on Python 3. That's where you are seeing the most energy and enthusiasm from Python developers.

Driscoll: What changes would you like to see in future Python releases?

Warsaw: I've been thinking lately about significant changes to the way we develop C extension modules. I'd like to see us get out of that business, by adopting something like Cython as the higher-level language and tool for generating extension modules. By doing this, we'd lay the groundwork for improvements in the C API, uncoupled from all the existing extension modules out there.

We'd be able to experiment with more internal changes that break the C API, such as removing the Global Interpreter Lock (GIL) or adopting a traditional garbage collector. If you look at the gilectomy work for example (that is, an experimental branch to remove the GIL), it's very complex, because it has to maintain compatibility with the existing C API as much as possible. If we could break that, without breaking source-level compatibility with third-party modules, we'd be much more free to improve things internally.

Driscoll: Thank you, Barry Warsaw.

10

Jessica McKellar

Jessica McKellar is an American software engineer and entrepreneur. She is a maintainer for several open source projects and the co-author of *Twisted Network Programming Essentials*. Jessica is a former director of the Python Software Foundation (PSF) and a former organizer of the Boston Python User Group. She is passionate about growing the Python community and serves as the diversity outreach chair for PyCon North America.

Jessica is the founder and CTO of Pilot, a bookkeeping firm which is powered by software. Previously, she was the founder and VP of engineering for Zulip, a real-time collaboration start-up which Dropbox acquired.

Discussion themes: Python and activism, the PSF, Twisted.

Catch up with Jessica McKellar here: @jessicamckella

Mike Driscoll: Could you give a little background about yourself?

Jessica McKellar: I'm an entrepreneur, software engineer, and open source developer currently living in San Francisco.

I am extremely proud to play a role in Python community initiatives. I joke that I don't ever take vacation because I just travel to speak at Python conferences. This has given me the opportunity to speak with and learn from local Python communities around the world.

> **Jessica McKellar: 'I am extremely proud to play a role in Python community initiatives.'**

I'm grateful to have won the O'Reilly Open Source Award in 2013 for my outreach efforts in the Python community. This was really recognizing the long-term efforts of many talented people, who I am also lucky to call my friends.

I'm currently a founder and the CTO of an early-stage enterprise software company, where I am delighted to have been using and benefiting from Python 3 from the get-go. Previously, I was a founder and the VP of engineering at Zulip.

Before that, I was a computer nerd at MIT who joined her friends at Ksplice, a company building a service for rebootless kernel updates on Linux, that was acquired by Oracle. These diverse experiences got me onto the Forbes 30 Under 30 class of 2017 for enterprise software, just in time to age out of the category.

Driscoll: So why did you first become a programmer?

McKellar: I had always liked using computers. A famous family photo shows me in front of an Apple IIci, with a bottle in one hand and a mouse in the other. But I didn't have any intentions around learning how to program until I was in college.

My first degree is actually in chemistry. While I was taking my chemistry classes, many of my friends were in the computer science department. I would sort of watch them out of the corner of my eye and think to myself that they seemed to be learning a toolkit full of tools for solving a broad range of problems in the world. I wanted those skills too.

I took a couple of CS classes in my sophomore year, was immediately hooked and secretly got a summer internship at a software company without telling my chemistry advisor (I don't recommend this tactic). I managed to cram a CS degree into my remaining couple of semesters.

Learning how to program is a profound experience. You become fluent within a system and learn how to break down and solve problems within it in a structured way. You gain confidence as a debugger and as a problem solver.

> **Jessica McKellar: 'Learning how to program is a profound experience...you gain confidence as a debugger and as a problem solver.'**

Contributing to free and open source software projects is also a profound experience. You are instilled with the mindset that if you see something that could be better, in a language, library or ecosystem, then you can work together with other contributors to make that change for everyone's benefit.

> **Jessica McKellar: 'Contributing to free and open source software projects is also a profound experience.'**

Believing that you have the tools to identify a problem in the world, break it down into steps, and work with others to implement a solution is a powerful mindset. It's an activist's mindset. Programming has profoundly impacted how I think about myself and my responsibility to my community. It has motivated my time on initiatives ranging from teaching programming to criminal justice reform.

> **Jessica McKellar: 'Programming has profoundly impacted how I think about myself and my responsibility to my community.'**

So I'd say that I learned how to program because I wanted the problem-solving toolkit that programmers have, but the most enduring effect is that it made me an activist. I have since devoted a lot of my energy to creating opportunities for others to learn how to program because we need as many people as possible, on this planet, to have the activist's mindset that programming encourages.

> **Jessica McKellar: 'We need as many people as possible, on this planet, to have the activist's mindset that programming encourages.'**

Driscoll: Why Python?

McKellar: I learned Python because that was the language used in many computer science classes at MIT. I was a student during a big transition from Lisp to Python at the university.

I've since used Python in every job I've ever had and in every company I've started. One should always use the right tool for any task, but Python has such broad utility and such a mature ecosystem, that it has fortunately frequently been the right tool.

Driscoll: How did your first start-up come about, Jessica?

McKellar: My first start-up was Ksplice, which came out of the master's thesis of our CEO, Jeff Arnold.

The Ksplice team had a ton of collective open source experience, which helped us to interface with the Linux kernel community. The experience and knowledge that we had in open source also shaped how we did software development in what came to be a highly distributed team.

Driscoll: Can you tell us how you became a director for the PSF?

McKellar: My Python community involvement started locally. I was working with the Boston Python User Group to run a series of introductory workshops for new programmers, as part of a diversity outreach initiative. I then became an organizer for Boston Python.

> **Jessica McKellar: 'My Python community involvement started locally.'**

The work became more global when I was invited to the inaugural cohort for the PSF's Outreach and Education Committee, which funded community building and educational initiatives in Python communities around the world.

At that point, I'm grateful that Jesse Noller, PSF's director, encouraged me to reach for an even larger platform for community building. He nominated me to become a director on the board. I was elected in 2012 and served for three years.

Driscoll: What was your focus as a director at that time?

McKellar: My focus was on global community development, including providing financial support, and a lot of organizational infrastructure for user groups, conferences and outreach initiatives.

Driscoll: What lessons have you learned as a core maintainer of Twisted?

McKellar: My first ever open source contribution was to Twisted, which is an event-driven networking engine written in Python!

I distinctly remember that formative experience. I was using Twisted in a project at an internship and I was using some documentation that I thought could be clearer. I said, "Hey, this is my chance to contribute to an open source project. I'm going to go for it."

I probably read through the contribution guidelines three times top to bottom. I was anxious that I might make a mistake and someone would yell at me. I remember idling nervously in the IRC channel, opening a new issue in the issue tracker, attaching a `diff` and generating and regenerating the docs to convince myself that everything looked perfect. I hovered my hand over the submit button for a solid minute before working up the nerve to click.

The outcome was that Glyph Lefkowitz, the creator of Twisted (and a decade later still a friend and coworker), patiently walked me through the review process. He landed my change and encouraged me to keep participating. I had an incredibly positive first experience of contributing to an open source project.

> **Jessica McKellar: 'I had an incredibly positive first experience of contributing to an open source project.'**

That ended up being a good investment for Twisted and for me, as I went on to contribute many more patches, become a core maintainer and write a book about the library.

The enduring open source lesson from Twisted has thus been about the importance of establishing a culture that welcomes new contributors. This is both because it is the right thing to do and because attracting and retaining a diverse contributor base is critical for sustaining a large open source project, on which many people and companies depend.

> **Jessica McKellar: 'The enduring open source lesson from Twisted has thus been about the importance of establishing a culture that welcomes new contributors.'**

Driscoll: Can you tell me more about Pilot, the company that you founded?

McKellar: Pilot is a bookkeeping firm (`http://pilot.com`). Unlike existing bookkeeping services, we are using software to automate the heavy lifting and a small team of pros to handle the rest. This results in books that are more accurate (less work and worry for you) and cheaper. It has been a delight to build this company on Python 3!

Driscoll: Thank you, Jessica McKellar.

11

TAREK ZIADÉ

Tarek Ziadé is a French Python developer and author. Past roles have included R&D developer at Nuxeo and software engineer at Mozilla. Today Tarek is a staff application engineer at Mozilla, where he creates tools for developers. He has written several Python books, in both English and French, including *Expert Python Programming* and *Python Microservices Development.* Tarek is the founder of Afpy, a French Python user group and has delivered talks at both PyCon and EuroPython. He regularly contributes to open source Python projects.

Discussion themes: AI, v2.7/v3.x, Afpy.
Catch up with Tarek Ziadé here: @tarek_ziade

Mike Driscoll: Why did you become a programmer?

Tarek Ziadé: In hindsight, I became a programmer for two reasons: to become the god of my little world and to impress my mom, who is a programmer as well.

When I was six years old, I was at a fair with my mom. There was a giant paper sheet on the floor, with a turtle that had a pen. You could program the turtle with cards to tell it where to go and when to put the pen down on the paper. I was obsessed with that turtle. The feeling of planning what would happen felt so good.

Years later, my mom got us a serious computer (the Thomson TO8D), and I could program in BASIC and Assembly. I built incredible things. With my mom's help, I was driving robots.

Driscoll: What sort of things did you do with the robots with your mom?

Ziadé: Well, the computer we bought had a programmable serial port and extensions to get a parallel port, which was quite rare back then.

We were driving step engines in BASIC or Assembly (with a cartridge), since the ports could be directly addressed. This was nothing fancy, but as a kid, being able to do at home something similar to what we were doing with that turtle amazed me.

My mom also got one of those fancy Olivetti laptops, with a small needles printer that could print stuff in three colors. We were having fun printing fractals. My mom was doing the heavy lifting (as a math teacher) and I was just tweaking the colors.

Driscoll: So how did you come across Python?

Ziadé: When I started coding professionally in the nineties, I was using Borland tools (C++Builder and Delphi) which could use VCL components.

My company bought some VCL components, but we were highly frustrated by the poor support from their authors and some bugs. That's when I discovered the Indy Project, which was developing and releasing open source VCL components that provided most network protocols. That library was to us, what Requests is to Python today.

> **Tarek Ziadé: 'Communities built around open source projects struck me as the way to go in software computing.'**

I got intrigued by this open source concept. Communities built around open source projects struck me as the way to go in software computing. Through my online research, I found out about the Zope Project and eventually discovered Python through that. A few months later, I joined a company that was building a Zope CMS.

Driscoll: Have you done anything with robots using Python?

Ziadé: Not really. I hacked a bit on a Raspberry Pi when I first got one. I also hacked a Wireless Ghetto Blaster using a suitcase, some old car speakers and a Raspberry Pi, with a Wi-Fi dongle and Mopidy.

> **Tarek Ziadé: 'I also hacked a Wireless Ghetto Blaster using a suitcase, some old car speakers and a Raspberry Pi.'**

I looked at the OpenCV library through Python to do some image processing. Most of the other electronics projects that I worked on were on Arduino and its pseudo C language. My most advanced project was a small RC car and that was about it. I got a little bit bored after that.

Driscoll: Python is big in AI and machine learning at the moment. What do you think makes Python so popular?

Ziadé: I think that Python has become popular for AI because the SciPy community has built some state-of-the-art frameworks and libs in the past few years (pandas, scikit-learn, IPython/Jupyter) that lower the bar for scientists to use Python instead of R or other tools.

> **Tarek Ziadé: 'AI and machine learning innovation is spearheaded by academics... Python becomes a natural fit for them.'**

AI and machine learning innovation is spearheaded by academics. Since Python has steadily grown as one of the main languages for learning programming in academics, Python becomes a natural fit for them.

Driscoll: What did you personally like about Python?

Ziadé: I fell in love with Python and its community. Python is open source, versatile, and powerful, yet simple to code.

Coming from a C++ and Delphi background, at first I thought that Python was a weak scripting language that could not be used to build serious applications. Eventually, I became impressed by how simple it was to create Python programs that were concise and straightforward to understand.

C++ and Delphi looked over-engineered at that point for all of the network applications that I was building. I could just write Python scripts that followed the KISS principle and build serious web applications that way.

Driscoll: What would you say are Python's strengths and weaknesses as a language?

Ziadé: Today, with over a decade of Python programming behind me, I think that Python's biggest strength is how visionary Guido van Rossum and the Python-Dev team are. As far as I can tell, every decision that was made in the last 20 years was a good one.

> **Tarek Ziadé: 'Python's biggest strength is how visionary Guido van Rossum and the Python-Dev team are.'**

From the memorandum (a CPython freeze designed so that other implementations like PyPy and Jython could catch up), to how asynchronous features were gradually added, Python got modernized in the right direction.

Each time that Python was getting a little bit behind compared to other languages, another feature would be added. Unlike some other languages that had a stellar start, then faded again, Python is steadily getting bigger every year.

One weakness for Python is the standard library. The fact that a package added in the stdlib is rarely removed is an issue. For instance, the stdlib currently has two classes named Future that are slightly different. One is in `asyncio` and one is in `concurrent`. I wish Python had a better story for its stdlib.

I think the biggest weakness of Python is the Python 2 versus Python 3 never-ending debate. That issue drove away some developers, because of the uncertainty about which version to use. It looks like we're getting past that debate now, which is great.

> **Tarek Ziadé: 'I think the biggest weakness of Python is the Python 2 versus Python 3 never-ending debate.'**

Driscoll: What is your opinion on the long life of Python 2.7?

Ziadé: I think that the transition took a while but it is happening transparently now and it is a success. The Python 2 versus 3 days are over, since the Python 3 ecosystem is now mature enough for most projects.

To my knowledge, there are no major libs or frameworks that are still lacking Python 3 support. So there's no good reason to start a new project using Python 2.7. People just use Python and for most of them it will happen to be Python 3. One day Python 2.7 will cease to exist and nobody will really miss it.

> **Tarek Ziadé: 'One day Python 2.7 will cease to exist and nobody will really miss it.'**

Driscoll: How did you end up becoming an author of Python books?

Ziadé: When I started programming in Zope and Python, I was the creator and maintainer of a French forum called Zopeur. I was spending a lot of time answering all of the questions.

Zopeur started as a one-man project, so if I stopped answering questions, then nobody else answered them. I was also learning so much by actually searching for answers and by diving into the details.

> **Tarek Ziadé: 'I was also learning so much by actually searching for answers and by diving into the details.'**

The first book that I wrote about Python came about because I wanted to dive deeply into Python and make my work useful to others. I was filling a gap too, since there were no original books in French about Python.

Driscoll: What have you learned in the writing process?

Ziadé: Writing a book is a long and exhausting project. The first book took me nine months and was very painful to finish. It's easy to quit. It's also common to get lost in details and forget about the big picture. I've learned how to organize my thoughts and keep the big picture in my head.

When I wrote my first book in English, I also learned the hard way that it's difficult to write in a non-native language. You need to keep your sentences as straightforward and short as possible. I was also exposed to a larger community of readers, for better or worse.

The last thing to note about writing books is that you need to accept that your book will never be perfect. By the time you have finished writing, and you have read back through the first chapters, you will want to rewrite things all over again.

> **Tarek Ziadé: 'You need to accept that your book will never be perfect.'**

Driscoll: Have you learned anything from your readers? If so, what?

Ziadé: I've learned a lot from feedback from my readers. I still get a few emails from readers wanting to share their thoughts.

Sometimes readers want to point out some mistakes or share solutions that they think are better. I have received a few interesting threads that I wish had been available to me before my books were published. I think books that are published on the web in real time, allowing readers to send feedback as the writer delivers chapters, are superior for that reason.

Driscoll: Are you aware of any other books about Python that have come out in French since yours were published?

Ziadé: To be fair, there was a Zope book before mine. But as far as I know, mine was the first book entirely dedicated to Python which was written in French, by a native speaker. Since then, there have been dozens of books written in French about Python. I am the old guard now.

> **Tarek Ziadé: 'Mine was the first book entirely dedicated to Python which was written in French, by a native speaker.'**

Driscoll: Why did you found the French Python User Group, Afpy?

Ziadé: As I mentioned earlier, I was maintaining a Zope/Python forum called Zopeur. At some point I had the idea of having a meeting in real life in Paris, with a dozen of the active members. We met for beers and we founded a foundation around Python. After that, I shut down my forum and we built Afpy on the ground.

Driscoll: What challenges did you face then and are there any challenges currently?

Ziadé: The first few years of running Afpy were great. We were all good friends united around our passion for Python.

The first challenge that we met was how to integrate French companies that wanted to be part of Afpy. That took us a few years, because enterprises wanted to use our foundation as a tool to promote their business (sometimes aggressively). We were risking losing the original spirit of Afpy.

> **Tarek Ziadé: 'We were risking losing the original spirit of Afpy.'**

We were also a bit paranoid about what would happen if several developers from the same company were elected to the steering committee. But when we started to organize PyCon France, it became a natural fit for those companies to be sponsors. In hindsight, I think that we did the right thing by being protective.

Another challenge was trying to have more diversity in Afpy. We were mostly men and I wanted to make our foundation more welcoming to women. I did some work around that and found that diversity was a very controversial topic. Eventually, I got burnt out from politics and the work was not fun anymore.

> **Tarek Ziadé: 'Eventually, I got burnt out from politics and the work was not fun anymore.'**

I was Afpy president for seven years, so I felt that it was the right time to move on. I am not sure what the current status of Afpy is, since I'm not involved. Afpy still looks like a vibrant user group though, which is great.

Driscoll: What made you choose Zope over some of the other alternatives?

Ziadé: The standard was PHP-powered frameworks back then, but Zope was the cool stuff. Zope was very innovative and with Python it was more than web pages.

> **Tarek Ziadé: 'Zope was very innovative and with Python it was more than web pages.'**

Plone was starting to take off and get very popular in France. Companies that specialized in building a CMS for government agencies often used Plone, because it had most features already built in. Plone, at one point, was at the top of the game for accessibility and groupware features.

Driscoll: Which Python web framework do you use now and why do you use it?

Ziadé: At Mozilla we do a lot of Django and Flask, and a bit of Pyramid. Occasionally we use some Twisted and Tornado. Since we're now shipping most stuff in Docker images, developers that start new projects are not tied to specific Python versions anymore. So asynchronous frameworks are starting to get used.

When I can pick my framework of choice, I like to use Bottle, for very simple web services and Flask, for bigger projects that need a bit of UI. There are a large number of Flask libraries out there. That said, the next server-side project that I will start will be `aiohttp`, that's for sure.

Driscoll: Are you working on any open source projects yourself that you would like to talk about?

Ziadé: I work on several projects, but a project that I am obsessed with right now is `molotov` (`http://molotov.readthedocs.io/`). It's a small load testing tool, based on Python 3.5+ and `aiohttp` client, that we're using to test our web services.

> **Tarek Ziadé: 'A project that I am obsessed with right now is molotov.'**

The design focuses on making it as straightforward as possible for developers to write a load test, by describing a scenario using simple Python coroutines. Once we have a set of those functions, then they are used to run simple smoke tests, load tests and distributed load tests.

Thanks to `asyncio` and `aiohttp`, the tool can send a pretty amazing load on our services and we're able to break most services with a single `molotov` client. I am adding on the top of this tool some CI Helpers, so we can continuously test the performance of our service.

One extension that I am going to add this quarter is the ability to deploy a stack with Docker images on AWS. This will happen prior to running the load test and grab back metrics once it's done. We also have a bigger project called Ardere, that drives AWS ECS for doing distributed tests. You can follow all of the work on those tools at `https://github.com/loads`.

Mike Driscoll: What are you most excited about in Python today?

Ziadé: Asynchronous programming. The addition of `async/await` in the language and projects like `aiohttp` are truly putting Python back into the game of building network apps. Of course, we have been able to do that with Twisted for over a decade, but now it's part of the core and implemented in a beautiful way. It's as easy as in Node.js to build async web apps in Python.

Driscoll: What changes would you like to see in future Python releases?

Ziadé: I'd love to see PyPy on a par with CPython (maybe we should have yet another memorandum so that PyPy catches up) and have the ability to run any of my projects with it (including C extensions). More anecdotally, I would love to see `setup.py` killed in our packaging system. It's the source of many issues. I've tried and failed (see PEP 390), but maybe one day it will happen.

Driscoll: Thank you, Tarek Ziadé.

12

SEBASTIAN RASCHKA

Sebastian Raschka received his doctorate in Quantitative Biology and Biochemistry and Molecular Biology in 2017, from Michigan State University. His research activities included the development of new deep learning architectures to solve problems in the field of biometrics. Sebastian is the bestselling author of *Python Machine Learning*, which received the ACM Best of Computing award in 2016. He contributes to many open source projects including scikit-learn. Methods that Sebastian implemented are being used in real-world machine learning applications such as Kaggle. He is passionate about helping people to develop data-driven solutions.

Discussion themes: Python for AI/machine learning, v2.7/v3.x.

Catch up with Sebastian Raschka here: @rasbt

Mike Driscoll: Could you give a little background information about yourself?

Sebastian Raschka: Of course! My name probably already gives it away, but I was born and raised in Germany, where I lived for more than two decades, until I had the urge to go on an adventure and study in the US.

I received my undergraduate degree from Heinrich-Heine University in Düsseldorf. I remember one day walking to the cafeteria and stumbling upon a flyer regarding a study abroad program with Michigan State University (MSU). I was super intrigued and thought that this might be a worthwhile experience. So not long after that, I studied for two years at MSU and received a Bachelor Plus/ International degree.

During those two semesters, I made many friends at MSU and thought that the scientific environment would provide an excellent opportunity for me to grow as a scientist, which is why I applied for grad school at MSU. I should say that this chapter of my life came with a happy ending, as I obtained my Ph.D. in December 2017. So that's my academic career.

> **Sebastian Raschka: 'During my time as a graduate student, I got heavily involved in open source in the context of data science and machine learning.'**

During my time as a graduate student, I got heavily involved in open source in the context of data science and machine learning. Also, I am a passionate blogger and writer. Some people may have stumbled upon my book, *Python Machine Learning*, which was very well-received by both people from academia and the industry.

With my book, I tried to bridge the gap between purely practical (that is, coding) books and purely theoretical (i.e., math-heavy) works. Based on all of the feedback that I received, *Python Machine Learning* turned out to be super useful to a broad audience. The book was translated into seven languages and is currently used as a textbook at the Loyola University Chicago, the University of Oxford, and many others.

Driscoll: Do you contribute to any open source projects?

Raschka: Yes, besides my writings, I am contributing to open source projects such as scikit-learn, TensorFlow and PyTorch. I also have my own little open source projects that I work on in my free time, including mlxtend and BioPandas.

mlxtend is a Python library with useful tools for the day-to-day data science tasks. It aims to fill the gap in the Python data science system, by providing tools that are not yet available in other packages. For example, the stacking classifiers and regressors, as well as the sequential feature selection algorithms, are very popular in the Kaggle community.

In addition, the frequent pattern mining algorithms, including Apriori and algorithms for deriving association rules, are super handy. Most recently, I added a lot of non-parametric functions, for evaluating machine learning classifiers from bootstrapping, to McNemar's tests.

> **Sebastian Raschka: 'To stay most productive, I didn't want to learn a whole new API for each little side project.'**

The BioPandas project arose from the need to work with molecular structures from different file formats more conveniently. During my Ph.D., many projects involved working with protein structures, or structures of small (drug-like) molecules. There are many tools out there for that, but each has its own little sublanguage. To stay most productive, I didn't want to learn a whole new API for each little side project.

The idea behind BioPandas is to parse structural files into pandas DataFrames, a library and format that most data scientists are already familiar with. Once the structures are in a DataFrame format, we can use all of the power of pandas that is at our disposal, including its super flexible selection syntax.

A virtual screening tool that I recently developed, screenlamp, makes heavy use of BioPandas as its core engine. I could screen databases with more than 12 million molecules efficiently, which led to the successful discovery of potent G protein-coupled receptor signaling inhibitors, with applications to aquatic invasive species control, in collaboration with experimental biologists at MSU.

> **Sebastian Raschka: 'Semi-adversarial networks are a deep learning architecture that I developed with my collaborators in the iPRoBe Lab at MSU.'**

Besides all of my involvement in computational biology, one of my other passion projects involves semi-adversarial networks. Semi-adversarial networks are a deep learning architecture that I developed with my collaborators in the iPRoBe Lab at MSU, which we successfully applied in the context of privacy concerns in the field of biometrics.

In particular, we applied this architecture to perturb face images in such a way that they looked almost identical to the original input images, while soft biometric attributes, such as gender, were inaccessible by gender predictors. The overall goal is to prevent nasty things like profiling, based on soft biometric attributes, without a user's consent.

Driscoll: So why did you become a programmer?

Raschka: I would say that the primary driving factor for becoming a programmer was to be able to implement my 'crazy' research ideas.

In computational biology, we already have many tools at our disposal that we can use without the need to program ourselves. However, using existing tools (depending on the research task) can also be a bit limiting. If we want to try something new, especially if we want to develop new methods, then there is no way around learning how to program.

Like most people, I started with simple Bash scripting in a Linux shell. At some point, I realized that this wasn't quite enough, or not efficient enough. During my undergraduate studies in Germany, I took a bioinformatics class in Perl.

When I saw what was possible with Perl, this was quite an eye-opening experience. Later, when I was conducting statistical analyses and preparing data visualizations based on the data that I collected, I also got into R. Not long after that, I got into Python.

Driscoll: Why Python?

Raschka: Well, I mentioned that I started with Perl and R. However, one thing that most programmers have in common is that we consult the internet on a regular basis to look for useful pointers, and other tips and tricks for achieving certain subtasks.

> **Sebastian Raschka: 'I stumbled upon many different resources that were written in Python and I thought that it would be worthwhile learning this language.'**

Suffice it to say, I stumbled upon many different resources that were written in Python and I thought that it would be worthwhile learning this language. At some point, I moved away from Perl entirely and did all of my coding in Python: custom scripts for data collection, parsing and analysis.

I also have to mention that I did all of the statistical analyses and plotting in R. Actually, not too long ago, when I was revisiting an old project, I stumbled upon my old Frankenstein-esque scripts (Bash scripts and makefiles), which were running Python and R in tandem.

Now, back in 2012, when the scientific computing stack was growing quickly, I stumbled upon NumPy, SciPy, matplotlib and scikit-learn. I realized that everything that I did in R, I could also do in Python. I could avoid switching back and forth between languages in my projects.

> **Sebastian Raschka: 'I really enjoy being part of and interacting with the vivid Python community.'**

Looking back, picking up Python was probably one of the best decisions that I made. Without Python, it wouldn't have been possible for me to be so productive. But besides research and work, I really enjoy being part of and interacting with the vivid Python community. Whether I am interacting with people via Twitter, or meeting people at conferences like PyData and SciPy, it's always a fun experience.

Driscoll: Python is one of the languages that is being used in AI and machine learning right now. Could you explain what makes it so popular?

Raschka: I think there are two main reasons, which are very related. The first reason is that Python is super easy to read and learn.

I would argue that most people working in machine learning and AI want to focus on trying out their ideas in the most convenient way possible. The focus is on research and applications, and programming is just a tool to get you there. The more comfortable a programming language is to learn, the lower the entry barrier is for more math and stats-oriented people.

> **Sebastian Raschka: 'I would argue that most people working in machine learning and AI want to focus on trying out their ideas in the most convenient way possible.'**

Python is also super readable, which helps with keeping up-to-date with the status quo in machine learning and AI, for example, when reading through code implementations of algorithms and ideas. Trying new ideas in AI and machine learning often requires implementing relatively sophisticated algorithms and the more transparent the language, the easier it is to debug.

The second main reason is that while Python is a very accessible language itself, we have a lot of great libraries on top of it that make our work easier. Nobody would like to spend their time on reimplementing basic algorithms from scratch (except in the context of studying machine learning and AI). The large number of Python libraries which exist help us to focus on more exciting things than reinventing the wheel.

> **Sebastian Raschka: 'The large number of Python libraries which exist, help us to focus on more exciting things than reinventing the wheel.'**

By the way, Python is also an excellent wrapper language for working with more efficient C/C++ implementations of algorithms and CUDA/cuDNN, which is why existing machine learning and deep learning libraries run efficiently in Python. This is also super important for working in the fields of machine learning and AI.

To summarize, I would say that Python is a great language that lets researchers and practitioners focus on machine learning and AI and provides less of a distraction than other languages.

Driscoll: Were there any moments where things may have gone another way, but surreptitiously ended up the way that they did?

Raschka: That's a good question. Maybe the fact that Python was popular among the Linux community, but worked very well on Windows as well. This was likely a big contributor to Python becoming so popular today.

There are relatively similar languages out there like Ruby. The Ruby on Rails project was (and still is) super popular. If projects like Django hadn't started, Python might have become less popular as an all-rounder, which may have led to fewer resources and open source contributions being devoted to developing Python. In turn, Python may have been less popular as a language for machine learning and AI.

> **Sebastian Raschka: 'If Travis Oliphant hadn't started the NumPy project...I think fewer scientists would have picked up Python as a scientific programming language.'**

If Travis Oliphant hadn't started the NumPy project (it was called Numeric back then in 1995), I think fewer scientists would have picked up Python as a scientific programming language early in their careers. We would all still be using MATLAB.

Driscoll: So is Python just the right tool at the right time, or is there another reason that it's become so important in AI and machine learning?

Raschka: I think that's a bit of a chicken or the egg problem.

To untangle it, I would say that Python is convenient to use, which led to its wide adoption. The community has developed many useful packages in the context of scientific computing. Many machine learning and AI developers prefer Python as a general programming language for scientific computing, and they have developed libraries on top of it, like Theano, MXNet, TensorFlow and PyTorch.

On an interesting side note, having been active in the machine learning and deep learning communities, there was one thing that I heard very often: "The Torch library is awesome, but it is written in Lua, and I don't want to spend my time learning yet another language." Note that we have PyTorch now.

> **Mike Driscoll: Do you think this opens the door for any Python programmer to start experimenting with AI?**

Raschka: I do think so! It depends on how we interpret AI, but regarding deep learning and reinforcement learning, there are many convenient packages with Python wrappers out there.

Probably the most popular example at the moment would be TensorFlow. Personally, I use both TensorFlow and PyTorch in my current research projects. I have been using TensorFlow since it was released in 2015 and like it overall. However, it is a bit less flexible when trying out unusual research ideas, which is why I recently got more into PyTorch. PyTorch itself is more flexible and its syntax is closer to Python; in fact, PyTorch describes itself as "a deep learning framework that puts Python first."

Driscoll: What could be done to make Python a better language for AI and machine learning?

Raschka: While Python is a language that is very convenient to use and nicely interfaces with C/C++ code, we have to keep in mind that it is not the most efficient language.

Computational efficiency is why C/C++ is still the programming language of choice for several machine learning and AI developers. Also, Python is not supported on most mobile and embedded devices. Here we have to distinguish between research, development and production.

> **Sebastian Raschka: 'The convenience of Python comes at a price, which is performance.'**

The convenience of Python comes at a price, which is performance. On the other hand, speed and computational efficiency comes with a trade-off in terms of productivity. In practice, I think that it's usually best to split tasks when working in a team, for instance, having people who specialize in research and trying new ideas, and people who specialize in taking prototypes to production.

I am mainly a researcher and haven't run into this problem yet, but I have also heard that Python is not good for production. I think this is mainly due to existing infrastructure, however, and the tools that are supported by the servers, so it's not really Python's fault per se.

> **Sebastian Raschka: 'Python doesn't scale as well as other languages such as Java or C++.'**

In general, due to its nature as a high-level and general-purpose programming language, Python doesn't scale as well as other languages such as Java or C++, although they are more tedious to use. For instance, spending too much time in the Python runtime, when working with TensorFlow, can be a real performance killer. Improving the general efficiency of Python (I don't think this is really possible though while keeping Python as convenient as it is) would be beneficial to AI and machine learning.

> **Sebastian Raschka: 'Improving the general efficiency of Python...would be beneficial to AI and machine learning.'**

While Python provides a great environment for rapid prototyping, it is sometimes a little bit too forgiving and dynamic types allow you to make mistakes more easily. I think the recent introduction of type hints may help to improve this issue to some extent. Also, keeping type hints optional is a great idea, because while it helps with larger code bases, it can also be an annoyance for smaller coding projects.

Driscoll: What are you most excited about in Python today?

Raschka: I am super excited that I can do anything that I need in Python. I can spend my time efficiently on research and problem solving, without the need to spend most of my days learning new tools and programming languages.

> **Sebastian Raschka: 'I am super happy with the status quo of Python. I am excited about the continued development of the fundamental data science libraries like NumPy.'**

Sure, sometimes it's good to look beyond the Python ecosystem, to see what's out there and what could potentially be useful. However, overall, I am super happy with the status quo of Python. I am excited about the continued development of the fundamental data science libraries like NumPy, which received a large grant from the Moore Foundation to focus on improving the library even further.

Also, I recently saw a conference talk on the redesign of pandas, pandas 2, which will make this already great library even more efficient, without changing the user interface.

The one thing I am probably most excited about, though, is the great community around Python. It's great to feel part of the Python community and to be in the same boat regarding advancing the landscape of tools and science. I can share knowledge, learn from others and share my excitement with likeminded people.

> **Sebastian Raschka: 'It's great to feel part of the Python community and to be in the same boat regarding advancing the landscape of tools and science.'**

Driscoll: What do you think about the long life of Python 2.7? Should people move over?

Raschka: That's a good question. Personally, I always recommend using the latest version of Python. However, I also realize that this is not always possible for everyone.

If your project involves working on or with an older Python 2.7 code base, then it may not be feasible to make the switch in terms of resources. Regarding the long life of Python 2.7, we all know that Python 2.7 will not be officially maintained after 2020. One thing that might happen is that a subcommunity will take over the maintenance of Python 2.7.

> **Sebastian Raschka: 'One thing that might happen is that a subcommunity will take over the maintenance of Python 2.7.'**

I also wonder whether it would be worthwhile to spend the energy and resources maintaining Python 2.7 after 2020 as a side project, versus taking the time to port Python 2.7 code bases over to Python 3.x. The long-term maintenance of Python 2.7 will always remain uncertain.

Personally, I always install the latest version of Python when it comes out and do all of my coding in Python 3. However, most of my projects also support Python 2.7. The reason is that there are still many people using Python 2.7 who cannot switch, and I don't want to exclude anyone. So if it does not require any major hassle or clunky workarounds, then I write my code in a way that is compatible with both Python 2.7 and 3.x.

> **Sebastian Raschka: 'There are still many people using Python 2.7 who cannot switch and I don't want to exclude anyone.'**

Driscoll: What changes would you like to see in future Python releases?

Raschka: My apologies, but my answer is a rather boring one: I am quite happy with Python's current set of features and don't have anything significant on my wish list.

One thing that I and multiple other people are sometimes complaining about is Python's Global Interpreter Lock (GIL). However, for my needs, it's typically not an issue. For instance, I like control over when to do multithreading or multiprocessing.

I wrote my little multiprocessing wrappers (in the mputil package) to evaluate Python generators lazily, which was an issue concerning memory consumption when I was working with vanilla *Pool* classes from Python's multiprocessing standard library. Besides, there are great libraries out there, like joblib, which make multiprocessing and threading super convenient.

On top of that, most libraries that I use for the heavy lifting when it comes to doing computations in parallel (Dask, TensorFlow, and PyTorch) already support multiprocessing and use Python more as a glue language as I mentioned earlier, so that computational efficiency is never really an issue.

Driscoll: Thank you, Sebastian Raschka.

13

WESLEY CHUN

Wesley Chun is an American software engineer who has worked at Google for the past eight years. In his role as a senior developer advocate, Wesley encourages developers to adopt Google tools and APIs. He previously worked for Yahoo! and was one of the original Yahoo! Mail engineers. Wesley is a fellow of the Python Software Foundation (PSF) and runs CyberWeb Consulting, which specializes in Python training and technical courses. He is the bestselling author of the *Core Python Programming* book series and co-authored *Python Web Development with Django.* Wesley has also contributed to Linux Journal, CNET, and InformIT.

Discussion themes: Yahoo! Mail, Python books, v2.7/v3.x.
Catch up with Wesley Chun here: @wescpy

Mike Driscoll: So why did you become a programmer?

Wesley Chun: I've been fascinated by the ability to write code to solve problems for a long time now. My interest probably started during the latter years of high school.

My programming teacher showed us how to write code implementing Gauss-Jordan elimination and have a computer solve systems of equations automatically. This demonstrated how code could be used to automate tedious work that previously required inefficient human power to compute.

While we were only using Commodore BASIC, being able to implement that algorithm and watch it work successfully, was one of the factors that motivated me to become a professional developer. Wanting to make people and processes more efficient has led to my multi-decade career as a software engineer.

> **Wesley Chun: 'Wanting to make people and processes more efficient has led to my multi-decade career as a software engineer.'**

Driscoll: So how did you come across the Python programming language?

Chun: Finding Python was not by choice. I had experience with C/C++ programming, as well as popular shell languages such as Tcl and Perl. Then I began working at a start-up company where Python became the primary development language. I learned Python and helped to build what was eventually to become Yahoo! Mail in the late 1990s.

Driscoll: How was Yahoo! Mail created?

Chun: In 1997, I was working at a start-up called Four11. True to its name, the first product released by the company was one of the first online versions of the telephone white pages directories.

The Four11 service, while being a web app, was written entirely in C++, a monolithic binary that was burdensome to build and cumbersome to maintain. The CTO and co-founder began to look for a way to develop more nimbly.

After researching a variety of scripting languages, the CTO discovered that if you left all of the hardcore work as C++, Python was a language that you could drop in as the front-end, as well as replace the middleware with.

Our next product, RocketMail, was developed with this modified stack. We created our own web framework before that term even existed. Using this framework, our core team was able to launch a successful mail service, which caused Yahoo! to acquire our company. RocketMail became Yahoo! Mail and the rest is history.

Driscoll: So how did you end up becoming an author?

Chun: Becoming an author was also accidental. During one of my summer internships at college, I was given the task of writing a user manual for customers.

I learned how to write using Ventura Publisher and with that experience under my belt, my coding and writing have been paired together ever since.

> **Wesley Chun: 'When I was exposed to Python in the workforce, there were only two Python books on the market.'**

When I was exposed to Python in the workforce, there were only two Python books on the market. One was a large case study book, while the other was the first Python book, which was already somewhat outdated. The need for a book about Python, for developers coming from languages like C and shell scripts, drove me to craft the first *Core Python Programming* book.

Driscoll: What have you learned from writing Python books?

Chun: If I wasn't already a developer, then I could probably say that I learned Python from writing books. Any time that you write a book, you need to do some research into the subject matter.

You should learn more information about your subject than is really necessary. In order to take a thorough look at a programming language, you must become familiar with both commonly-used features and corner cases.

Driscoll: How have your readers impacted your writing?

Chun: Having readers come up to me and let me know that I was one of their primary sources for learning Python, always brings a smile to my face.

> **Wesley Chun: 'Readers come up to me and let me know that I was one of their primary sources for learning Python.'**

Whenever possible, I ask for direct feedback from my readers so that I can make my books even better. Readers love the exercises after a chapter, which help to reinforce what they learned. They also appreciate the wide variety of topics covered.

Driscoll: Could you explain the idea behind CyberWeb Consulting?

Chun: Yes, my home business is meant to consolidate all of the freelance work that I perform for the Python community. CyberWeb Consulting incorporates magazine articles, the technical Python training courses that I teach and other Python-related consulting opportunities that come my way.

Driscoll: What projects are you working on now?

Chun: To this day, I still help people to discover how mundane and laborious tasks, which were once performed by humans, can now be automated. This frees people up to have higher pursuits.

> **Wesley Chun: 'I still help people to discover how mundane and laborious tasks, which were once performed by humans, can now be automated.'**

I'm currently a developer advocate at Google. I show developers how to integrate Google technologies into their apps, web or mobile. I started by advocating Google Cloud Platform products, but have since moved to the familiar G Suite productivity applications: Gmail, Google Drive, Calendar, Sheets, etc.

While people are familiar with these well-known apps, I focus on teaching programmers about the developer platforms and APIs behind each of those tools. You'll often find me on the G Suite Developers blog or hosting the G Suite Developer Show (`http://goo.gl/JpBQ40`).

On the Python side of the house, I'm working on the third edition of *Core Python Programming*, which was my first book. Readers familiar with *Core Python Programming* will know that the book is being broken up into two volumes. The third part of the second half, *Core Python Applications Programming*, was published back in 2012. Now I'm writing the third edition of the first half. This latest book will be called *Core Python Language Fundamentals*, to better reflect its content.

I also have a Python blog, which I've honestly been neglecting. Fortunately for me, work has provided content for the blog because any of my work on Google developer products features a good deal of Python code.

Driscoll: What most excites you about Python at the moment?

Chun: Believe it or not, I'm most excited that people even know what Python is today. Back in the old days, nobody had ever heard of Python before. Python was such a great tool, so we hoped that the world would one day find out about it. I think we're there now.

> **Wesley Chun: 'Python was such a great tool, so we hoped that the world would one day find out about it. I think we're there now.'**

I'm also excited that we are near the end of the crossroads of having both Python 2 and 3. Python 3 adoption has taken off and most packages are now available.

Driscoll: What do you think about the long life of Python 2?

Chun: Soon Python 2 will be in the rear-view mirror. Those who are skeptical of Python 3.x may remain that way, but that group is slowly disappearing. Python moving from 2 to 3 is not the same as moving from Perl 5 to 6.

The long life of Python 2 was necessary because of the backwards incompatibility of Python 3. However, Python 2.6 and 2.7 are great migration tools. They are the only 2.x versions that have 3.x features backported to them, to help with the overall migration.

> **Wesley Chun: 'I proclaimed that it would take a decade for the world to move to Python 3, due to its lack of compatibility with Python 2.'**

I have been writing and speaking about the longevity of Python 2 for some time. Back in 2008, when 3.0 launched, I proclaimed that it would take a decade for the world to move to Python 3, due to its lack of compatibility with Python 2.

Based on the momentum that I'm seeing today, I think that I'm going to be more accurate in my prediction than I thought was possible. My original statement was mostly a flippant and abstract one, which has gradually become more concrete and realistic over the past few years. But Python 3.6 is a great version to move over to!

> **Wesley Chun: 'I think that I'm going to be more accurate in my prediction than I thought was possible.'**

Driscoll: Python is being increasingly used today for AI and machine learning. Why do you think this is?

Chun: Python makes a great language, regardless of the field that it is applied to. Python does not require its users to be computer scientists in order to be able to solve problems. The language syntax does not get in the way for those who want a tool to build solutions with. Python is also great at encouraging group collaboration because of its understandable syntax.

Driscoll: So how do you think that Python could be made a better language for AI and machine learning?

Chun: The continued development of existing Python libraries and the creation of new libraries would make working in the AI field even easier. That would help everyone.

> **Wesley Chun: 'The continued development of existing Python libraries and the creation of new libraries would make working in the AI field even easier.'**

Driscoll: What changes would you like to see in future Python releases?

Chun: I'd love to see fewer Python releases and fewer new features. I think what the language has today (Python 3.6) is great.

> **Wesley Chun: 'I'd love to see fewer Python releases and fewer new features.'**

Sure, we need to have bug and security fixes. Additional performance improvements would also be welcome, along with the solving of the Global Interpreter Lock issue. However, I'd like to see the release schedules stretched out.

Eventually, I'd like to see development mostly stop with Python, so that it could be recognized as a standard like C or C++. If further improvements need to be made, then they can come as revisions to the standard. Being recognized as a standard will bring about Python's legitimacy and its greater adoption, especially in larger corporations.

Driscoll: Thank you, Wesley Chun.

14

STEVEN LOTT

Steven Lott is an American software developer and author. He is an associate for the bank holding company Capital One and uses Python to build APIs for new products. Previously, he worked as a solution architect for CTG, which provides IT services. In 2003, Steven started using his talent for solving problems with Python to write books. He has since authored titles including *Modern Python Cookbook*, *Python for Secrets Agents*, and *Functional Python Programming*. Steven creates educational content for the Python community and writes a tech blog.

Discussion themes: Python pros and cons,
Python books, v3.6.
Catch up with Steven Lott here: @s_lott

Mike Driscoll: So why did you become a programmer?

Steven Lott: I started programming in the 1970s, when computers were rare. My school had two Olivetti Programma 101 calculators and an IBM 1620 computer.

It was empowering being able to create useful behavior on these machines, such as simulating random events, drawing things and trying to design new kinds of games. A responsive and autonomous device was the ultimate toy, even when doing math homework. The idea of building things that were new and useful via software was compelling. Also, I had a bunch of friends who hung around in the computer room.

Driscoll: How did you start using Python?

Lott: In the late 90s, as object-oriented programming was building momentum, I started tracking the popular languages.

I had a Macintosh with the port of Smalltalk-80, the THINK C++ compiler and a JDK 1.1. I made regular searches for emerging object-oriented programming technology and eventually found Python.

> **Steven Lott: 'The barriers to entry for Python were so much lower than the other languages that I had learned.'**

The barriers to entry for Python were so much lower than the other languages that I had learned. There was only a runtime and no complex toolchain required to build software. Python was replacing Perl, AWK, sed, and grep with one tool that handled a variety of use cases. By 2000, I was trying to build useful and working applications in Python.

Driscoll: What did you like about Python?

Lott: At first, I was drawn to the elegant simplicity of Python. The standard library provided an amazing array of tools. As I learned more, the vast ecosystem of modules and packages outside of the standard library showed me how much could be done.

I used Python at work because I could solve a problem quickly. The language was wonderful for complex data wrangling problems. In many cases, success stemmed from getting started quickly and discovering the nuances and complications of a problem as early as possible. Python encourages you to fail quickly and start again on a new course.

> **Steven Lott: 'Python encourages you to fail quickly and start again on a new course.'**

The more that I learn about NumPy, the more that I see Python as a kind of universal container for code. The NumPy libraries are based on C (and Fortran), so having a Python wrapper makes them widely available and useful.

The underlying reason for using Python wasn't clear to me until Guido van Rossum's keynote speech at PyCon 2016. Python's biggest strength stems from the community. Python's open source nature creates and encourages a community effort to build cool new things.

> **Steven Lott: 'Python's biggest strength stems from the community.'**

Python has numerous other strengths, such as its wide adoption as a language. Python is used in numerous contexts: scientists are using it to analyze truly gigantic datasets and it's used to build scalable web services too. Python is also used recreationally by home hackers who are integrating their Alexa, Nest, and Arduino-based temperature sensors.

Another strength of Python is sometimes called *batteries included.* With a single download, you have all the tools you want. If you want to learn the language, then you can start with the distribution for your computer. If you want to do data science, then you can start with the Anaconda distribution, which is where lots of packages are bundled.

The Python Software Foundation (PSF) makes active steps to be as inclusive as possible. The philosophy is that everyone should be able to learn and share their findings. Python's community believes that nobody should be excluded. We're all using Python to solve problems, so we all need help.

Driscoll: What are Python's weaknesses as a language?

Lott: I've collected a few lists of Python's weaknesses. Some of them are utterly farcical and I've seen many sentiments which make no sense at all. A few complaints about Python are meaningful.

Overall, I've learned that most problems that are blamed on the Python language being slow are more often than not due to ineffective algorithm and data structure choices.

> **Steven Lott: 'Python's core runtime is remarkably fast.'**

Python's core runtime is remarkably fast. Fortran and C are considerably faster because they have optimizing compilers, that produce code focused on the underlying chipset. The SciPy and NumPy use of binary code wrapped in Python addresses this concern nicely.

Another issue is the opportunity for confusion when using Python. The orthogonality between language statements and data structures means that lists, sets, and dictionaries have some overlapping features. The immensely sophisticated implementation of Python data structures makes it possible to make a bad choice and get correct answers, but have horribly inefficient code.

Lastly, a weakness for Python is the possibility of creating inheritance problems. Everything is dynamic, so it can be difficult for tools like Pylint to discern meaningful method redefinitions from spelling mistakes with similar-looking method names and plain bad design.

The `collections.abc` module has decorators that can be used to organize code and provide some help with checking redefinitions. The type definitions in the `typing` module allow mypy to locate potential problems.

Driscoll: So how did you end up becoming an author of Python books?

Lott: Most roles in my career more or less just happened to me, but becoming a writer was a conscious decision.

In this case, I had decided that there could be value in teaching the Python language and the associated software engineering skills. I started to collect notes for a book in 2002. By 2010, I had tried self-publishing several books on Python.

> **Steven Lott: 'Over a few years, I answered thousands of questions about Python and somehow built up a large reputation.'**

When Stack Overflow started, I was an early participant. There were many interesting Python questions. The questions showed gaps where more information was needed about Python specifically and software engineering in general. Over a few years, I answered thousands of questions about Python and somehow built up a large reputation.

Driscoll: What have you learned in the writing process?

Lott: I've learned about the difficulty of creating meaningful and interesting examples. An example needs to have a story arc and a problem that requires a solution.

Stories require drama and conflict, and that doesn't often surface when thinking about data structures and algorithms. I spend more time wandering around trying to think of examples than doing any other part of the writing process. A lot of the problems that I come up with are too large and complex.

A snippet of code is difficult to describe if it doesn't solve a problem.

For example, the traveling salesman problem has a compelling story arc that characterizes graph traversal. Having a story provides a framework for remembering the essential problem and seeing how the solution works. Pure code doesn't help anyone to understand why the language construct is important. Code only exists to solve a problem, so it's imperative to describe the problem.

> **Steven Lott: 'Pure code doesn't help anyone to understand why the language construct is important. Code only exists to solve a problem, so it's imperative to describe the problem.'**

Creating stories requires the time to view the problem from a distance, which is essential for summarizing and abstracting out needless details. Finding the right details requires a deep understanding. I know that I've failed when the description of the code becomes long and complex, involving tangential topics.

Driscoll: What are the pros and cons of self-publishing your books versus using a regular publisher?

Lott: The difference between self-publishing and using a publisher is editing. The way that Python handles documentation testing (via the `doctest` module) means that the technical aspects of the content can be validated automatically. I've become better at this, but there are still some testing gaps in my published code.

Other challenges are grammar, usage, clarity, precision, color, unity, coherence, and concision. With Packt Publishing, there's a pipeline of editors who ask questions and notice the incomprehensible parts, long before my book lands in the hands of a reader.

When I self-published, I did what seemed best to me. Publishers manage costs, prices, and revenue streams adroitly. My job is to know Python and Packt Publishing handles the rest.

Driscoll: Have you learned anything from your readers? If so, what?

Lott: My readers have taught me the importance of using the Python `doctest` tool for checking each example in the body of a book. Readers have spotted numerous errors from code that I didn't check properly.

Driscoll: What has been your favorite interaction with a reader?

Lott: I work for a tech company in Northern Virginia. A co-worker was surprised to find out that I'd written *Mastering Object-Oriented Python*. They had bought the book based on recommendations and read the outline, without really looking at the author's name.

Driscoll: So which of your books has been the most popular? Why do you think that people buy one book over another?

Lott: My most successful book has been *Python for Secret Agents*. It seems like the fun factor is part of that. If a book has a wide variety of fun exercises and problems, then readers can see how Python applies to the problems that they know and want to solve. If the book is too narrowly focused on one problem domain, or too abstract, then the practical applications become hard to envision.

Driscoll: What new and exciting trends are you seeing in Python?

Lott: Python 3.6 is fast and getting faster. The developers working on foundational algorithms have done impressive things.

> **Steven Lott: 'Python 3.6 is fast and getting faster. The developers working on foundational algorithms have done impressive things.'**

The new internal data structures for the `dict` save memory and run faster. This kind of internal re-engineering is exciting. There are huge benefits that come from having an upgrade with few visible changes to the language.

Another exciting direction that Python is going in is connected to the mypy project and the type hints. You have a handy quality tool that doesn't involve a profound change to the language, or the development tools. This can help you to write more reliable code, without introducing significant overheads. If mypy becomes part of Pylint or Pyflakes, then that will help even more.

As an Arduino maker, I often collect data for later analysis using Python-based tools. My current project involves a customized GPS tracker, which will be used on a boat to monitor its position while at anchor. An alarm will sound when the vessel is drifting. There are numerous other examples of Internet of things (IoT) projects, where Python is an important part of the overall effort to build something new and useful.

Driscoll: Do you see Python becoming a popular language for embedded programming now that MicroPython is becoming popular?

Lott: Yes, MicroPython and the pyboard are exciting new developments. Raspberry Pis also run Python nicely.

> **Steven Lott: 'MicroPython and the pyboard are exciting new developments.'**

Processors continue to become faster and smaller, which means that more sophisticated languages can be used. One of the first computers that I ever used had 20K of memory and was the size of an upright piano. My first Apple II Plus had 64K of memory and covered the top of a desk. A pyboard has 1M of ROM and 192K of RAM in a package which is just over two square inches.

Driscoll: Thank you, Steven Lott.

15

Oliver Schoenborn

Oliver Schoenborn is a Canadian software developer and independent software developer. Past roles have included working as a simulation consultant at CAE Inc and as a visualization software developer at the National Research Council Canada. Oliver is passionate about connecting with the business and government communities. He is the author of Pypubsub (hosted at `https://github.com/schollii/pypubsub`), a Python package that gives users a simple way to decouple parts of their event-based application. Oliver regularly updates Pypubsub and contributes to the wxPython mailing list.

Discussion themes: Pypubsub, Python in AI, Python's future.

Catch up with Oliver Schoenborn here: @schollii2

Mike Driscoll: So let's start with your background. Why did you decide to become a programmer?

Oliver Schoenborn: Well, a buddy at school was selling his Apple IIe. I had never done programming before that, but I decided to buy his used computer. I was 14 at the time.

I remember being quite intrigued by the BASIC and assembly language. There was a command prompt and you could somehow drop into the assembly level to write assembly. I read the many manuals for the computer, which described how to program it. I tried to write some little programs and eventually got into Pascal. I really enjoyed it.

In my fifth year of high school, a school teacher asked us to do something with a language called Logo. It was basically graphics commands to move a pen right, left, draw lines etc. I created a simulation loop in there so that I could simulate a little aircraft flying and dropping a bomb. It was very simple but it was fun, and the teacher was impressed!

So that's how I got into programming. It was more or less a chance in some ways. At that point, programming was still just a hobby, because my goal was to get into physics.

Driscoll: So how did you end up getting into Python itself?

Schoenborn: At work we had a project that needed some graphical user interface development on Windows.

For the previous 10 years, I had mostly programmed in C++ on UNIX, developing command line and 3D graphics applications, but not menu-based applications (except for a GUI written in Java AWT). I really dreaded MFC, so I started looking into options on Windows for doing that. I came across Python (because it was platform independent), and Tk.

> **Oliver Schoenborn: 'Python was the perfect fit. As soon as I saw the language, I really related to its simple and clean syntax.'**

Python was the perfect fit. As soon as I saw the language, I really related to its simple and clean syntax. I don't know if it just matched my way of thinking. I also found wxPython and saw that its API seemed to be rather solid. I fell in love with Python and the ability it provided to quickly create interfaces using wxPython.

So how I got into Python was through a work project that had requirements that were more easily achievable in Python than in C++.

Driscoll: Was this how you got involved with the wxPython community as well?

Schoenborn: That's right. I developed my first application in wxPython as a result of that project. It was an application for analyzing seat heating and air-conditioning. Back then, automobile seat comfort was being prototyped using this kind of software.

So I used wxPython and I thought that the publish-subscribe pattern that it supported was a really awesome idea. I got involved more heavily with the wxPython development by taking over the Pubsub component of that library.

> **Oliver Schoenborn: 'I got involved more heavily with wxPython development by taking over the Pubsub component of the wxPython library.'**

Driscoll: So was Pubsub started by someone else?

Schoenborn: Yes, Robb Shecter created the first version of Pubsub. There were limitations that I needed to get around (mostly, a memory leak: subscribers were not released after they were no longer needed by the application), and I proposed some significant patches and unit tests. Robb was looking for someone to take over `wx.lib.pubsub`. So I did that.

Driscoll: Is that also when Pubsub got split into its own module away from wxPython?

Schoenborn: I think it was a couple of years later. Pubsub was pretty much a standalone sub-package, whereas most other wx.lib sub-packages required other wxPython components. I wanted to make wx.lib.pubsub available to a broader set of developers, and others on the wxPython developers group agreed.

> **Oliver Schoenborn: 'Pubsub was pretty much a standalone component.'**

Driscoll: Were you guys aware of the PyDispatcher projects at that time?

Schoenborn: Well, I did become aware of PyDispatcher at some point in those years. It was quite a different approach.

I remember that at the time it was not topic- based. Pubsub was sufficiently different from it to be justified as a separate package. It has been a while since I have looked at it, but it would be interesting actually to see where PyDispatcher is at now.

There are several projects now that use the basic idea of topics, messaging, and publish/subscribe (such as MQTT and Google pub/sub), but at the network, that is the inter-application level, whereas Pypubsub is at the application inter-component level. They have evolved much more than Pubsub has had to evolve; Pypubsub is mature and production quality.

Driscoll: So I noticed that when you did that interview with me in the PyDev of the Week series, you had switched to PyQt. How did that happen?

Schoenborn: That was some time in 2013. We basically had this project that involved modernizing an old prototype that our client had. The application involved user-defined scripts that could be run by the prototype and those were all written in Python. So we had to either embed a Python interpreter, or translate huge Python scripts into another language, while guaranteeing the same outputs, (a task that could not fit within the scope of the project budget).

> **Oliver Schoenborn: 'We had to either embed a Python interpreter, or translate huge Python scripts.'**

The graphics interface had to be very sophisticated. At the time, the prototype had a 3D component, where the user could rotate model components in a 3D environment. We needed to integrate the graphical user interface with menus and list views as a sophisticated 2D and 3D canvas, where the user could interact with things.

We wanted something that was stable, powerful, and well-documented, with an active community behind it. At the time, WPF, wxPython, and PyQt (or Qt, for a C++ infrastructure) were the main candidates for us. On the C# side there was WPF. We looked at a number of different approaches and in the end it was between wxPython and PyQt.

PyQt seemed to have more powerful integration of a 3D environment than wxPython did. PyQt also seemed to be quickly growing towards supporting a 3D scene graph, whereas in wxPython I would have had to use OpenGL, and this would have been more complicated.

Python 3 was required, but I think that's when Robin Dunn decided to create wxPython 3, and so the work on supporting Python 3 was still very early. Basically, there was only Python 2.7 for wxPython and the availability of Qt Designer was also a factor. PyQt had a very sophisticated interface for creating designs.

> **Oliver Schoenborn: 'PyQt definitely seemed to have momentum.'**

An XML-driven user interface description was supported by both PyQt and WPF.

PyQt definitely seemed to have momentum, and it supported commercial use of the package, which was important for that project. I had had some negative experiences with WPF, fighting with the black-magic that it used in order to bind properties to widgets. Also, there were signs that IronPython was unmaintained. All things considered, we picked PyQt. We did not regret the choice.

Driscoll: Going back to the Pypubsub part, I forgot to ask you, did you have any challenges while running that open source project that you'd like to talk about?

Schoenborn: Well, it wasn't really a technical challenge, but I did have an interesting experience from an open source development point of view. It reminded me that you don't really control the space that you can occupy in the open source world.

> **Oliver Schoenborn: 'You don't really control the space that you can occupy in the open source world.'**

What happened was that Pypubsub was on SourceForge, where it was named simply "pubsub", because that's how it was named in wxPython. On PyPI I had named it pypubsub. A couple of years later, I found out that there was another project on SourceForge called Pypubsub, but it hadn't gone anywhere. Basically, it was a dead project and sometimes it led to some confusion on Stack Overflow and the two pypubsub forums.

That took some effort to straighten out. I had to contact the author and explain what was going on. Eventually, he agreed and I was able to take ownership of the "pypubsub" name on SourceForge.

In the meantime, GitHub had become really popular. Some people had copied my Pypubsub source code into GitHub, just to have it handy. Nothing wrong with that, but since these forks were not to add features, when I actually decided to move Pypubsub to GitHub, I had to let some devs know that Pypubsub was finally available there. I explained that there probably was no longer a good reason to have separate copies. This was an interesting aspect of open source.

Driscoll: How much of a commitment was the project?

Schoenborn: Well, there have been various periods during the past 15 years when I made major changes to the implementation and extended the API: fixing bugs, updating documentation, and make sure that all tests work when there was a new release of Python. Finding the time to do those things was often a challenge. It is, I guess, another interesting aspect of working on a volunteer basis.

Evolving the API, while maintaining backwards compatibility, was mostly requested by Robin, the wxPython author, and this was important to me even if Pypubsub was technically separate from wxPython. It was a major technical challenge to make that possible. This led to the concept of Pubsub supporting three APIs or messaging protocols.

> **Oliver Schoenborn: 'It was a major technical challenge.'**

First, there was backwards compatibility with the very first version of Pubsub. That was what I called the version 1 messaging protocol. Then there was the sort of "modern" Pubsub, which had significant improvements in the API, and there were two APIs for that.

One was called `arg1` because all message data was in one big blob given as one argument to the `sendMessage()` function. The other was called `kwargs` because message data was sent via keyword arguments in the `sendMessage()` function. That was the default when you installed Pypubsub standalone.

A vanilla installation of wxPython would install the `arg1` API, since that one was almost 100% compatible with the version 1 API. A setup flag could be set in the application code, before importing Pypubsub, to choose the `kwargs` protocol..

So getting all that to work was a major headache. I had to sort of hijack the import system a little bit, basically to allow for the user to say, "Well in this application I want the `arg1` protocol and in this wxPython application, I want the `kwargs` protocol.."

I also added some code to help transition a wxPython application from version 1 to `arg1`, to `kwargs` protocol. That was tough too.

I really wish that I hadn't had to do all that, but I felt at the time that it was a necessary evil.. Other than code complexity, it made the import system used by Pypubsub rather complicated, which could interfere with freezing.

Driscoll: Why did you focus on making this transition possible?

Schoenborn: Because I had to go through that challenge in one of my own applications on a project. It was using the `arg1` protocol and migrating it to the new `kwargs` protocol. Although not complex, this was somewhat tedious and error prone. It was worth adding these error checkers and going through the transition, due to the advantages of the `kwargs` API.

I had the concept of a parameter that you could set when you imported Pypubsub. This would configure Pypubsub to do some "in-between" tasks, that were useful during a transition between the two messaging protocols. The bridge would allow you to gradually move towards being fully kwargs, with some helpful facilities along the way.

> **Oliver Schoenborn: 'The code was certainly more complex than I wanted it to be.'**

Getting to a stable API took quite a bit of effort. The frustration was that the code was certainly more complex than I wanted it to be, so it was a harder to maintain and harder to trace calls through Pypubsub. Also, it caused some challenges for people who wanted to freeze their application.

As soon as I was able to, I suggested we deprecate all of that old stuff, since it was only useful for the wxPython app with the old API. Robin agreed. In 2016, I dropped all support for version 1 and arg1 protocols, allowing for a major clean up and the simplification of the code base. So now there's just one API. This is v4 of Pypubsub.

Driscoll: So can you tell me about some other Python projects that you've been involved with lately?

Schoenborn: Sure, one is a really cool closed-source project, which is very challenging technically, with a very sophisticated GUI. I actually mentioned it indirectly in discussing the reason for working with PyQt in recent years.

The application shows a canvas on which you can drop boxes and connect them together in different ways. The difference from a tool like Visio is that the user can program these boxes to change in time, like an animation, to represent a process.

The user does this by defining Python scripts. The application adds a live Python namespace to each user script, so that the user can dynamically query the underlying model (such as code completion on properties dynamically changed in the model).

> **Oliver Schoenborn: 'The application adds a live Python namespace to each user script, so that the user can dynamically query the underlying model.'**

So there's a very sophisticated interface for creating model components, adding them, and linking them. There is also a very sophisticated undo function that covers all the different aspects of model editing.

> **Oliver Schoenborn: ' As usual, there was 10% of the feature that occupied 90% of its dev time.'**

We coupled the view to the undo/redo so that the user could always see what was going to be undone, or redone, as they navigated their document. This was an interesting challenge, and as usual, there was 10% of the feature that occupied 90% of its dev time.

The application is a simulation system, so it's not just creating lines or boxes. There are interface components to manage the simulation, that is, the changing of the model in time, restoring it to its initial state, seeing the queue of changes, etc.

So there is a very large set of functionality in the application. But PyQt has been awesome to work with in that respect.

Driscoll: Could you explain a little more about using Qt for this project?

Schoenborn: Yes, Qt's Graphics View has been really impressive in terms of what it has allowed us to do.

I remember in the beginning, it was not always obvious how to do certain things in Qt. For example, in a canvas-based application, where you can do so many different things, it's super useful to have a state machine to manage what can be done at any given moment. There is no documentation that explains this because it is something that you learn over the years as a useful technique. Note that Qt has built-in support for state machines, but it wasn't sufficiently powerful for our needs.

A state machine allows you to define states in which only certain actions are possible. So in the "creating line" state, the only thing you can do is cancel creation, drag the mouse, or select the line target. That's where the state machine shines. Without it, your code ends up an unmaintainable spaghetti. Troubleshooting and extending with new actions is so much simpler.

Although the Qt docs are excellent, there are things you figure out as you go. Sometimes you say, "Oh yeah, I finally understand how to do this. I'm going to backtrack a bit and fix things." You end up with a more robust implementation that can really support the next level of features.

> **Oliver Schoenborn: 'You end up with a more robust implementation that can really have the next level of features.'**

I'm starting to get kind of familiar with all of the widgets that Qt has. There was a nasty bug that we found, when we upgraded PyQt, that caused a whole interface to show all sorts of lines as you dragged pieces around. Needless to say, that was a problem, but we really needed to update PyQt for other features.

We traced the problem back to the C++ layer and by some incredible stroke of luck, there was a workaround: there was one line of code that we just had to put in our application at Python level. We didn't even need to change the PyQt source code. As long as we had that one line of code, then the bug would go away. I submitted: `https://bugreports.qt.io/browse/QTBUG-55918`.

Another very interesting aspect of using Qt was unit testing. We needed unit tests for the GUI side of the application. We used the excellent pytest, and had one test suite for the core business logic, and one for the GUI components. Unit testing a GUI can be really challenging: you have to script user actions.

Luckily, Qt makes this relatively easy, in that you can easily trigger any widget event just by calling a method. But being event based, we needed a way to define a bunch of user actions, with the expected outcome. So I created a library to support doing this. Unfortunately, source is closed, so I could not share the code, but I mentioned the idea on the PyQt forum and some people implemented their own concept of it.

Driscoll: Python is one of the major languages being used in the AI and machine learning boom. What do you think is behind this?

Schoenborn: I would say that it's the "Olympian" nature of Python that makes it good for AI and machine learning. Python happens to be very strong in many of the necessary elements, instead of just one or two.

> **Oliver Schoenborn: 'It's the "Olympian" nature of Python that makes it good for AI and machine learning.'**

For example, Python can be used for functional, procedural, or object-oriented coding, in any combination, and the code is still understandable and clean. Moreover, no compilation needed makes the exploration of algorithms and data so easy: you just modify the code and re-run the script.

Finally, Python provides powerful abstractions using a simple syntax. Maybe I'm biased, but I think that Python is at the top in this respect. I'm big on explicit and clean code, and on refactoring and testing. Being strong at all of these things makes Python the perfect language for AI.

Mike Driscoll: What could be done to make Python a better language for AI and machine learning?

Schoenborn: A language is most useful, in a given problem domain, when the abstractions provided match those of the problem domain.

So if deep learning uses neural networks, then having a generic concept of a neural net could be really useful.. This is currently provided by libraries like TensorFlow. But perhaps as machine learning algorithms improve, a generic abstraction for a neural net will emerge that can become a basic data structure like lists and maps.

Also, I think we need the ability to ask the AI/machine learning functions, "How did you get to this result?" That's how humans validate conclusions. They are aware of the logic they used, they can verbalise it, another person can follow it, and they can verify its correctness.

Driscoll: Many people I have talked to, and even people at PyCon, have put a lot of emphasis on Python growing in the data science field. Are you seeing that in what you're doing, or can you give me any kind of opinion one way or the other?

Schoenborn: Yeah, Python is really growing in that field. Tools like Jupyter, Anaconda, and scikit-learn are major reasons for this, in my opinion.

Probably in combination with the fact that with large compute power, the speed of the language no longer matters so much. Python can be used in embedded systems, so in principle some predictive analytics based on trained machine models can happen in the devices themselves.

> **Oliver Schoenborn: 'With large compute power, the speed of the language no longers matters so much.'**

There was a really interesting presentation at PyCon in 2017. A presenter was surveying the plotting libraries landscape. The survey started with matplotlib and everything around that. Then the survey moved on to some of the JavaScript libraries, in some cases related to Python libraries. So this was really fascinating, because there is a lot of interest, even for my own clients, in using pandas, NumPy, and matplotlib. This showed that there are many different extensions or layers that you can add.

Speaking from a client perspective, you want a certain amount of capability and you don't want to be limited to only matplotlib, because there's so much more that's available. You also know that you don't want to be reinventing the wheel, so you must make sure that what you build is sufficiently generic. If you want to do statistical analysis, then you might want to do it with Jupyter or R. You always try to get a sense of the applications that are providing these capabilities.

You don't want to force the user to use matplotlib, because it is so diverse and the API is so advanced. There's no way that you can provide a GUI component that supports everything that matplotlib can do.

Python is such an expressive language and so easy to learn. I think that's why Python is so big now in research and applied research. It's easy to apply, sophisticated and solves technical problems.

> **Oliver Schoenborn: 'Python is such an expressive language and so easy to learn. I think that's why Python is so big now in research and applied research.'**

Python gives you all of the tools to make and provide something that's robust and deterministic. We can measure performance, find bottlenecks or find memory leaks. There are so many things that really make Python a great tool.

Driscoll: Have there been any other particularly memorable PyCon presentations?

Schoenborn: There was another interesting PyCon 2017 presentation about the Global Interpreter Lock (GIL). In theory, getting rid of the GIL would be so great: we could run Python threads on separate cores.

> **Oliver Schoenborn: 'In theory, getting rid of the GIL would be so great.'**

But the GIL solves a very practical problem: synchronizing access to Python data structures. You start digging into the GIL by analyzing what would be necessary, and what would be the gain versus the cost. You realize that the GIL really simplifies a lot of things and may well be a reason that it's so easy to do complicated things with Python.

You can basically get concurrent programming, without all the catches of multi-threaded programming. Most often in a large class of problems, that's what you want. In the other class of problems, you want to tackle trivially parallelizable problems. It's basically where you are subdividing the solution into tasks. There's very little coupling between the tasks and you can do it very easily.

Monte Carlo is one example because it's very important in simulation and business processes. You basically want to run a large number of things many times, with very little variation between them. Python makes that easy too.

For trivially parallelizable problems, you need to run those. You can run them on separate cores, just using a multiprocessing module. Yes, there's even that capability! So many different things that are complex in principle, are simple in Python, which makes it so usable for number crunching tasks.

> **Oliver Schoenborn: 'So many different things that are complex in principle, are simple in Python.'**

But I do think that there should be an easier way to run Python code on multiple cores without having to use the module. There should be language constructs that work hand in hand with the GIL. There is no technical infeasibility there; it's just that there has to be enough concerted effort to make it happen.

Driscoll: What are you most excited about in Python today?

Schoenborn: The optional type annotation system, asynchronous calls, and the multiprocessing module.

Driscoll: Which language is Python's biggest competitor would you say?

Schoenborn: JavaScript. It's just so unfortunate that JavaScript dominates the web side of things. There are these two major contenders: JavaScript on the web and Python in technical computing. If you really need the raw compute speed, then you can do C++.

You can get major speedups in Python, by writing some C++ code and ingesting it in Python via SWIG and SIP. There is also Cython. It's so easy to work at a high level of abstraction with Python, with that compute power when you need it from C++.

I don't know where that's going to go. I think that a lot of things would have to happen on the JavaScript side to make it as powerful and as simple to use as Python, but on the other hand, I can't see Python becoming a supported language in the web browser, because JavaScript is just too established. Maybe if Google decides to make Python code runnable from Chrome.

> **Oliver Schoenborn: 'A lot of things would have to happen on the JavaScript side to make it as powerful and simple to use as Python.'**

Driscoll: So is Python here to stay?

Schoenborn: I think that Python is here to stay. Python is too good a language and its community has developed good quality and solid libraries, and language evolution processes via PEPs. There is a very rigorous process for Python and a lot of smart people working on it. So it's here to stay for sure.

Driscoll: What do you think about the long life of Python 2.7? Should people move over to the latest version?

Schoenborn: The long life of Python 2.7 is most irritating! Big influencers, like Ubuntu and Google Cloud Platform, must start making Python 3.6 their default.

> **Oliver Schoenborn: 'The long life of Python 2.7 is most irritating!'**

Driscoll: What changes would you like to see in future Python releases?

Schoenborn: I would like to see an optional static typing system with type inference (so types do not need declaration), true parallelism, and an optional compilation mode.

The combination of optional static typing, compilation, and type inference would allow the language to stay simple when starting, and get more rigorous when needed.

It could also provide massive gains in speed and productivity: it's always a time saver to be able to point to any object and know exactly what operations are either available on it, or required of it (within a function signature). Realistically, I don't know if a compilation mode (even JIT) that freezes types is feasible, but there are some incredibly smart people out there, so I would not discount it.

With regards to parallelism, I'm referring to the ability to run Python code on multiple cores simultaneously, while keeping the GIL. Sure, there is the multiprocessing module, but I'm talking about constructs built into the language itself as first-class citizens.

Driscoll: Thank you, Oliver Schoenborn.

16

AL SWEIGART

Al Sweigart is an American software developer and the creator of two cross-platform Python modules: Pyperclip, for copying and pasting text, and PyAutoGUI, for controlling the mouse and keyboard. He is a successful author who has published four books on Python programming and a book on Scratch, a programming language for children. Al's books teach beginners how to code and he is passionate about helping young people and adults to develop programming skills. Al focuses on making programming knowledge more accessible and regularly speaks at Python conferences.

Discussion themes: Python books, Python packages, v2.7/v3.x.

Catch up with Al Sweigart here: @AlSweigart

Mike Driscoll: So how did you become a programmer?

Al Sweigart: I was a kid who loved the 8-bit Nintendo. Then a friend of mine found a book in the elementary school library about programming games in BASIC. I was hooked.

I sort of hate telling people how I got into programming, because I was one of those people who started when they were a young kid. I worry that telling my story makes people think, "Oh no, I haven't been programming since I was three weeks old, so it's too late for me. I'll never catch up!"

> **Al Sweigart: 'If anything, programming has become so much easier than it was 20 years ago.'**

If anything, programming has become so much easier than it was 20 years ago. We didn't have Wikipedia and Stack Overflow back then. I think everything that I learned about programming between the third grade and graduating high school, anybody could now learn in about a dozen weekends.

Most of my programming knowledge was drawn from that one book. I tried to make sense of the reference manual that came with my family's Compaq 386 computer. I couldn't understand that manual at all. I ended up never making anything as impressive as the Nintendo games I played.

Driscoll: So how did you end up moving into Python itself?

Sweigart: I first picked up Python around 2004. I was looking at making some web apps, and I was mostly programming in PHP and Perl, when a friend pointed out Python to me.

At that time, I wanted to learn as many different programming languages as I could, and Python was really nice. I loved the readability of the language. Everything that I used to do in Perl, I started doing in Python. I never found a programming language that I liked better after that, so I just stuck to Python and now it's been over a decade.

I sometimes feel that I need to actually force myself to learn different programming languages, just to stay on top of things. But Python has become my go-to language. Whenever I have to write a quick script or automate some really short task, it's easy to use Python.

Then again, it's really hard to predict the future and I've stopped trying. For instance, I really thought that something would come along to replace JavaScript, but if anything, it's just getting more popular! That, and I originally thought that including cameras in cell phones was a silly idea. So I've learned not to try to predict the future.

> **Al Sweigart: 'It's really hard to predict the future and I've stopped trying.'**

Driscoll: Python is playing a major role in the AI and machine learning boom. Can you explain that?

Sweigart: Well, not to fawn over Python too much, but what makes Python great for AI are the things that make it great as a language in general.

> **Al Sweigart: 'What makes Python great for AI are the things that make it great as a language in general.'**

Python is easy to learn and easy to use. It turns out that for most applications this is what's important. "Powerful" is a meaningless term when it comes to programming languages, because every language describes itself as "powerful".

Theoretically, there's no calculation that one language can do that another language can't. In practice though, you need a human programmer to take the time to sit down and write the actual code. A language that makes that easy to do is the one that will see more adoption, a larger community, and more libraries. So it doesn't surprise me that Python takes the lead in something like machine learning, where so many of the tools were developed recently.

Driscoll: What made you decide to start actually writing books about the Python language?

Sweigart: In 2008, my girlfriend was a nanny for a 10-year-old kid. He wanted to learn how to program, but he didn't really know where to start. I tried to find something on the web for him, but so much of the content back then was aimed at professional software developers.

So I started writing a tutorial, which eventually became *Invent Your Own Computer Games with Python.* I didn't want to bury the reader with programming concepts and technical jargon. I just wanted to list the source code to a game and then explain how its code worked. I kept adding more games and eventually it ballooned into book length. I self-published it, but also put it on the web for free under a Creative Commons license. People seemed to like it, so I went on to write *Making Games with Python and Pygame.*

There's a little cipher program in *Invent Your Own Computer Games with Python.* I thought putting a bunch of these classic ciphers together would make a good book. I'd explain not only how to write code to perform the encryption, but also how to break the encryption. These ciphers are from ancient Roman times, up to the 16th century, so the average laptop today has more than enough computing power to break them. That book became *Cracking Codes with Python.*

After I wrote that third book, writing turned into what I did with all of my spare time. There came a point where I could take a chance, leave the software developer job that I had, and write full-time. That worked out pretty well.

> **Al Sweigart: 'I came up with the right idea for a book, at the right time, and also for the right language.'**

I thought that I'd go back to another developer job after a year or so of writing, but *Automate the Boring Stuff with Python* completely blew me away with its success. It was mostly luck. I came up with the right idea for a book, at the right time, and also for the right language. So a lot of things just fell together.

Driscoll: Why did you decide to self-publish?

Sweigart: No Starch Press had approached me about publishing *Invent Your Own Computer Games with Python*, but that plan had fallen through.

I had this half-edited manuscript, so I finished editing it and turned it into a PDF to put on Amazon. All the promotion I did was online. I'd tell people about it on forums. People didn't see it as spamming because the PDF was also completely free to download.

Driscoll: Do you think that the success of *Invent Your Own Computer Games with Python* was due to having the book as a PDF, or as a web page?

Sweigart: I still think putting the book online for free, with a Creative Commons license, led to more people buying the book. People could see the book and generate word of mouth. There were other benefits too. With the book online, I could take a look at the traffic and see which chapters were getting the most attention.

> **Al Sweigart: 'The most popular chapters... were on GUI automation, web scraping and regular expressions. So when PyCon had calls for talk proposals, those were the topics that I chose.'**

The most popular chapters on the *Automate the Boring Stuff with Python* site were on GUI automation, web scraping, and regular expressions. So when PyCon had calls for talk proposals, those were the topics that I chose. That's how I started speaking at the regional PyCons and then at US PyCon in 2017.

I've noticed that the most popular topics in my books are not always the stuff that I think is the most interesting. I remember that when I was writing *Automate the Boring Stuff with Python*, I thought that the chapter on image manipulation would be popular. But it turns out that most people don't need to generate their own image files from Python scripts as much as I do.

> **Al Sweigart: 'I've noticed that the most popular topics in my books are not always the stuff that I think is the most interesting.'**

Driscoll: What have you learned as an author?

Sweigart: It's going to be more work than you think! A lot of people email me and say, "Oh hey, I'm interested in writing a book on programming. Do you have any advice for me?"

I don't know what to tell them. I'm a software developer by training. I know what I did and that my approach worked for me. But that's like a lottery winner advising you on which numbers to pick. *Automate the Boring Stuff with Python* did far better than my other books. I'm not really sure how well I could reproduce those results for someone else.

My most recent book was *Scratch Programming Playground*, which uses the Scratch programming tool, from the MIT Media Lab, to teach programming concepts to kids. That book is doing modestly well, but unfortunately the audience for Scratch isn't as large as the audience for Python.

I did learn that writing is something you have to do to get better at it. Actual practice is better than any advice I could give. Also, I learned that good editors are worth their weight in gold.

Driscoll: So what would you do differently if you could start over with one of your other books that didn't do so well?

Sweigart: I mean, if we're talking about the first book, then my biggest mistake was not writing it for Python 3. Originally, I was just using Python 2, because that's what I knew.

I didn't start questioning that decision until someone said, "Hey, why don't you use Python 3?" There really wasn't a particular reason not to, so I made the switch to Python 3 for *Invent Your Own Computer Games with Python*. That turned out to be a really smart thing.

> **Al Sweigart: 'I made the switch to Python 3 for Invent Your Own Computer Games with Python. That turned out to be a really smart thing.'**

Another big mistake when writing *Invent Your Own Computer Games with Python* was that I originally had the entire text just as HTML, because I was making it as a web tutorial in a text file. I was writing unit tests and using linting tools just to make sure that everything was formatted well. That turned out to be a large headache.

What I should have done is use Microsoft Word. A lot of people are really surprised when I tell them that, but Word and Excel are the two best things to come out of Microsoft. If I could send a message 10 years back in time, I'd tell myself to use real desktop publishing software.

Driscoll: Why did you choose Scratch, rather than one of the other children's beginner languages?

Sweigart: Scratch is the best programming tool for kids that I've encountered. A lot of programming tools for kids are dumbed down to the point that I don't feel like they're actually teaching programming.

Scratch made a lot of smart design decisions and teaches real programming, while hiding the messy details. Everyone interested in teaching kids to code should read the Scratch white paper by Mitch Resnick and also watch his TED talk.

Driscoll: So I want to change topic here slightly. Why did you create the Python packages Pyperclip and PyAutoGUI?

Sweigart: Pyperclip and PyAutoGUI both came out of needs that came up while I was writing programming books.

> **Al Sweigart: 'Pyperclip and PyAutoGUI both came out of needs that came up while I was writing programming books.'**

In *Cracking Codes with Python*, you're dealing with encrypting and decrypting text. Often, you're working with a lot of random nonsense text that you need to reproduce exactly, and having a copy-and-paste mechanism makes that much easier. It lets the user put the output into an email, or save it in a document. So I thought, "Well, how do you copy-and-paste text in Python?" There were some modules on PyPI that did copy-and-paste, but they would only work on one operating system, or they only worked for Python 2.

I wanted to have one module that worked on all operating systems, and also worked for Python 2 and Python 3. All I needed was a copy function and a paste function. I didn't think it would turn out to be much work, but of course it was. Fortunately, the user doesn't have to see all the messy details that went into making Pyperclip work on so many platforms. They only see a module with two functions.

Driscoll: So how did you get started on this idea of one module?

Sweigart: I didn't want readers to have to deal with picking different modules depending on what their computer setup was.

I combined all of that code into one module, to become Pyperclip, because I noticed that there was nothing on PyPI that did that. PyAutoGUI was created for similar reasons. I wanted to have a chapter on GUI automation for *Automate the Boring Stuff with Python*, but all the existing modules on PyPI were for different operating systems and worked differently.

> **Al Sweigart: 'The way that PyAutoGUI came about was because of this need to have one module that just worked.'**

The way that PyAutoGUI came about was because of this need to have one module that just worked. I think that's the main reason that PyAutoGUI is the most popular open source project that I've ever started. It's useful to a wide range of people.

Driscoll: What do you think should be the goal for anyone creating Python packages?

Sweigart: If you want to create a Python package, or any software, the most important thing is that it's easy to use.

> **Al Sweigart: 'If you want to create a Python package, or any software, the most important thing is that it's easy to use.'**

Before I even start writing any code, I just type out what the API would be like and how I would use it myself. I think a lot of programmers just like writing code and solving technical problems, but they don't realize that all of that is worthless if it's too complicated for people to actually use.

> **Al Sweigart: 'When starting out, the algorithms you write don't have to be elegant. You don't even need the code to be perfectly clean.'**

When starting out, the algorithms you write don't have to be elegant. You don't even need the code to be perfectly clean. As long as using the module is simple, then that's what gets people paying attention. Once you know you've made something that works, and that people want, then you can clean up the code for future development.

> **Al Sweigart: 'I'm always thrilled that many people use Pyperclip and it isn't just a toy that I created for myself.'**

I'm always thrilled that many people use Pyperclip and it isn't just a toy that I created for myself. I've learned a lot about making software that fits other people's needs. For example, with PyAutoGUI, I received bug reports from people with non-English keyboards or non-English language settings. These were issues that I would have never thought of if I was the only one using my creation.

It's given me an appreciation for just how much effort goes into making code that is robust enough for a wide and diverse set of users. I've made a few other open source projects, but Pyperclip and PyAutoGUI are the ones that taught me the most about writing software for other people.

Driscoll: Are there any other major insights that you've learned from operating these popular open source projects?

Sweigart: I've learned that, for the most part, people are really nice. I've heard some stories from open source maintainers about rude people demanding that you fix the bug they're encountering right then and there. But the people I've communicated with are really welcoming and even-handed about their criticisms. I really appreciate that.

Driscoll: What advice would you give to anyone who is reluctant to share their code online?

Sweigart: The sooner you put your code online and get people looking at it, the better.

You have to get over that fear of criticism, because I know code reviews have made me a better software developer more than anything else. You're missing out on so many opportunities to improve if you don't put yourself out there, and you can always post under an alias anyway.

> **Al Sweigart: 'The sooner you put your code online and get people looking at it, the better.'**

It's a lot like going to the gym. Sometimes people go to the gym and they're worried that everybody else is watching and judging them. But the other people at the gym are too busy thinking about themselves to notice them. I think the same thing applies to code. Most people don't actually read your code. I'm pretty sure that most technical recruiters who contacted me, never actually took the time to go through the hundreds of lines of code that I had out there already.

I tend to hate any code that I wrote more than two weeks ago. I look back on it and see so many mistakes and rough edges. A lot of programmers are like that. If you're worried that your code is too unpolished to post online, then at least you're in good company.

Driscoll: So do you have any specific advice for someone who wants to create the next big open source package in Python?

Sweigart: There's something called the Nobel Prize effect, which is when scientists win a Nobel Prize and then think, "What could I do to win a second Nobel Prize? I need to work on an even greater problem."

Then they set their sights way too high and never accomplish anything again. I sometimes feel that way about Pyperclip and PyAutoGUI because I didn't imagine they would become as popular as they did.

My GitHub profile has a ton of other repos that nobody has paid much attention to. So my advice would be to keep working on different ideas that you have. It's really hard to predict what's going to become popular. This was the case with the open source projects that I've created, but also with the books that I've written. I really had no idea that the successful things that I've worked on would be successful. Most of the things that I've worked on have not been successful at all.

Start small and keep growing. Learn from your mistakes and realize that you will make a lot of them. Put your code out there for criticism and learn to work with others, because all the big open source projects are made by teams, not by individuals. I think that's probably the best recipe for success.

> **Al Sweigart: 'All the big open source projects are made by teams, not by individuals.'**

Driscoll: What are you most excited about in Python today?

Sweigart: It seems like we're finally turning a corner when it comes to Python 3 adoption and for good reason.

There have been efficiency improvements to several places in the language and most notably to dictionaries in 3.6 (which are at the foundation of much of Python itself). The asyncio module seems like it could become a killer feature. But mostly I'm just excited that Python is being used by more people outside of software engineering like hobbyists, academics, and data scientists.

Driscoll: What do you think about the long life of Python 2.7? Should everyone move to Python 3 now?

Sweigart: Yes, absolutely people should move to Python 3. In 2018, the excuse that modules don't support Python 3 yet isn't true and hasn't been true for years.

The only reason to continue to use Python 2 is if you have a large existing codebase of Python 2 code, which, since Python had so much popularity early on, is unfortunately the case for a lot of codebases. But I feel at this point that there's been too many improvements to Python 3 to ignore.

> **Al Sweigart: 'I feel at this point that there's been too many improvements to Python 3 to ignore.'**

The better handling of Unicode strings was the selling point for me personally. I've seen a lot of code that just falls over the instant that someone uses non-ASCII characters in a string somewhere. I always thought it was odd that the versions before Python 3 were so awkward when it came to Unicode characters, until a friend pointed out that Python mostly predates Unicode. It's easy to forget how long Python has been around.

Driscoll: So where do you see Python going as a language? What features do you see coming in, or which fields do you see Python opening up in?

Sweigart: Python looks out at the programming landscape and weeps because there are no more worlds to conquer.

> **Al Sweigart: 'Python looks out at the programming landscape and weeps because there are no more worlds to conquer.'**

That's an exaggeration, of course. But it's amazing how many different areas Python is used in. It's a great general scripting language, but it's also used in massively scaled systems. It's used for web apps, but also machine learning. It's used by the largest tech companies, but also in high school computer science classes.

I'm trying to think about areas where Python hasn't been so successful. Embedded devices is one area, but MicroPython is addressing that as well. Python is a hard sell for triple-A gaming and VR, but it's great for hobbyist game makers and even a few indie game developers. Python is used for web app backends, but JavaScript is still the king of the frontend. I would love to see Python in the browser.

I've been a big fan of the changes in Python 3, if anything just because Python 3 got strings to finally work sensibly. A lot of programmers in the English-speaking world forget that ASCII is not a universal code. In fact, ASCII is not even universal in English-speaking countries. The original ASCII character set has a dollar sign, but not a British pound symbol. Writing code that won't break when somebody submits a string with accented letters is a huge win.

> **Al Sweigart: 'The Python community itself is the best community in tech that I've ever found.'**

What makes me optimistic about Python isn't the language itself, so much as the people behind it. The Python community itself is the best community in tech that I've ever found. They care about being open and inclusive, and that attracts a lot of new blood and fresh eyes. So I still think that Python has a lot of steam, even though it's been around for close to 30 years now. I think that Python is going to be relevant and sticking around for quite some time yet.

Driscoll: Thank you, Al Sweigart.

17

LUCIANO RAMALHO

Luciano Ramalho is a Brazilian software engineer and a fellow of the Python Software Foundation (PSF). He is a technical principal at ThoughtWorks, a design software company. Luciano previously taught Python web development in the Brazilian banking, media, and government sectors. He is the author of *Fluent Python* and served as a council member for the Brazilian Python Association for four years. Luciano regularly speaks at international Python conferences. He co-owns Python.pro.br, a training company and co-founded Garoa Hacker Clube, the first hackerspace in Brazil.

Discussion themes: Python books, APyB, v2.7/v3.x.
Catch up with Luciano Ramalho here: @ramalhoorg

Mike Driscoll: Could you give a little background about yourself, Luciano?

Luciano Ramalho: Sure, I'm a self-taught programmer. I was born in Brazil in 1963. When I was 15 years old, in 1978, I saw the Lunar Lander game running on a HP-25 calculator and became excited about the possibilities of combining programmable calculators and board games, which were my main geek passion at the time.

Later that year, my father's employer gave him a TI-58 calculator, which I promptly borrowed and never returned. My first interesting program was a port of the Lunar Lander from the HP to the TI language (both were assembly-like languages).

In 1981 I spent a year as an exchange student in Harrisburg, IL, and I was one of two volunteers that taught ourselves to program on the Apple II computers that the high school library had just received; no one else in the school knew what to do with them.

After I came back to Brazil, my first job was translating Apple II software manuals to Portuguese, and my second job was teaching programming, which became a lifelong passion for me.

> **Luciano Ramalho: 'My second job was teaching programming, which became a lifelong passion for me.'**

Since then, I've spent about half of my time being a programmer and half of my time being a teacher. I worked as a programmer for 8-bit educational software, CP/M standalone business apps, Windows client-server apps, Windows and macOS CD-ROMs, and on backend systems running on Unix for some of the earliest web portals in Brazil.

I had a couple of small companies (a desktop publishing bureau, a software house and a training company) and now I am proud to be a principal consultant at ThoughtWorks.

Today, the kind of programming that I like to do the most, is example code to illustrate new concepts in languages, APIs, and platforms. I'm very interested in DX (developer experience) as well. I really enjoy the challenge of coding the simplest example that can demonstrate an idea and still be interesting (not just `foo` and `bar` abstractions). That's why I call myself *a stand-up programmer*.

Driscoll: Why did you become a programmer?

Ramalho: I became a programmer because I enjoy programming as much as I enjoy playing board games.

I see a very strong parallel: the keywords and functions provided by a language are like the playing pieces and other game resources at your disposal, which you must arrange to achieve the desired effect. The language semantics are like the game rules. If a language has syntactic macros, then that's like being able to create completely new pieces during a game - a very powerful ability.

> **Luciano Ramalho: 'I became a programmer because I enjoy programming as much as I enjoy playing board games.'**

Besides being fun, programming lets us have a huge impact in the world, and I try to always have a positive impact.

Driscoll: Why Python?

Ramalho: I learned more than a dozen languages before Python, and I've studied at least half a dozen after it. But Python is the one that I've used for the longest time throughout my career.

Python fits my brain, as the saying goes. I find it elegant yet practical, simple but not simplistic, consistent but not rigid or limiting. After a while, I also made many friends in the Python community, so that became a huge reason to stick with it, even when sometimes I longed for something different.

I stumbled upon Python in 1998 when I was learning the OO features of Perl 5, which I'd been using for web development. At the time, whenever someone in the Perl mailing lists asked about the OO-way of doing something, comparisons to Python came up. After two or three such mentions of Python, I decided to look it up.

> **Luciano Ramalho: 'I read Guido van Rossum's tutorial and fell in love with the language. It combined the best qualities of Perl and Java.'**

I read Guido van Rossum's tutorial and fell in love with the language. It combined the best qualities of Perl and Java, the two languages that I was using most at the time. Python was a *real* OO language with a decent class library, like Java, but it was also concise and practical, like Perl, and more readable, consistent, and pleasant to use than both. I think that Python is a masterpiece of language design.

Driscoll: What do you think makes Python such a good language for AI and machine learning?

Ramalho: The most important and immediate reason is that the NumPy and SciPy libraries enable projects such as scikit-learn, which is currently almost a de facto standard tool for machine learning.

The reason why NumPy, SciPy, scikit-learn, and so many other libraries were created in the first place is because Python has some features that make it very attractive for scientific computing. Python has a simple and consistent syntax which makes programming more accessible to people who are not software engineers.

Another reason is operator overloading, which enables code that is readable and concise. Then there's Python's buffer protocol (PEP 3118), which is a standard for external libraries to interoperate efficiently with Python when processing array-like data structures. Finally, Python benefits from a rich ecosystem of libraries for scientific computing, which attracts more scientists and creates a virtuous cycle.

Driscoll: What could make Python a better language for AI and machine learning?

Ramalho: The biggest challenge for AI and machine learning projects in Python is deploying to production with all of the external dependencies required by such projects. Containers help a lot, but it's never easy.

Driscoll: How did you become an author, Luciano?

Ramalho: *Fluent Python* was the fourth book that I started, but the first that I finished. Writing a book takes a lot of time and it's easy to underestimate the required effort.

In 2013, I submitted a talk proposal for OSCON and was accepted. While I was at the conference, I approached the O'Reilly booth with four slides of a presentation on my iPad: book title, about me, and two slides of outline. They were interested and sent me the template for a book proposal. A couple of months later, I had signed a contract and got a small advance.

I worked on the book part-time initially. During that time, Meghan Blanchette, the editor, was the only person reading it. She gave me some very valuable guidance, especially with the flow of the book.

About nine months into the project, the first deadline was approaching and I would not make it. The O'Reilly contract included a clause that allowed a co-author to be imposed if I had a problem delivering. But *Fluent Python* was a very personal project for me, so I decided to quit all of my other freelance engagements and just focus on the book.

I worked for another nine months, probably around 50 hours a week, and finished it. During that second half, the tech editors joined the project. The reviewers were all people that I admire: Alex Martelli, Anna Ravenscroft, Lennart Regebro, and Leonardo Rochael. Victor Stinner focused on the chapter about asyncio, which was a new topic for the rest of us. They all gave me a lot of excellent feedback and encouragement.

Driscoll: What did you learn from writing *Fluent Python*?

Ramalho: I learned a lot about Python. While writing, I explored parts of the standard library that I had never visited before.

I grokked uniquely Pythonic language features like attribute descriptors and `yield from` expressions. I finally discovered why a Python program on Windows has no problem printing to cmd.exe console, but crashes with `UnicodeEncodeError` when its output is redirected to a file.

I learned a lot more about Python. I also learned the value of being yourself. Being passionate about a subject and knowing it well are good foundations for creating content.

> **Luciano Ramalho: 'I also learned the value of being yourself. Being passionate about a subject and knowing it well are good foundations for creating content.'**

I'm an avid reader, which is essential for writing. I am also very opinionated about language design. As a reader, I had been annoyed by technical authors who mixed facts and opinions in their writing, so I came up with the idea of the Soapbox sections at the end of each chapter. I could offer my opinions, while also making it clear to readers that they could skip that part. The Soapboxes were fun to write, and several reviewers enjoyed them as well. So that's an example of how being myself worked very well.

The Python community is made up of people who love to share what they know, and they deserve credit. So I kept notes of all the important references that I used during the book, including not only other books, but also blog posts, videos, and even StackOverflow answers. I shared these notes with readers in the *Further Reading* sections. That is also a feature of the book that some reviewers have praised.

> **Luciano Ramalho: 'The Python community is made up of people who love to share what they know, and they deserve credit. So I kept notes of all the important references.'**

On a personal level, writing *Fluent Python* and witnessing its success in reviews and sales was great for my self-esteem, after I had failed at writing a book on three prior attempts. So I guess one lesson is that it pays to persevere and go all-in when you believe in a project.

Some readers have offered me a lot of great feedback, and the most prolific of them became a good friend: Elias Dorneles. So another lesson is the importance of being open to feedback, and offering people the opportunity to give it.

Driscoll: What would you do differently if you could start over?

Ramalho: I'd write a shorter book! My original plan was to write 300 pages, but in the end it came to 770.

Alternatively, I could have written five shorter books, because each part of *Fluent Python* from II to VI works pretty well independently. But the resulting volume set would have been more expensive for readers, and perhaps would not have resulted in the same level of recognition and sales.

I have no regrets, because I've come to believe that whatever happens is the only thing that could have. I learned this from author Bruce Eckel, as one of the rules for open space events.

> **Luciano Ramalho: 'Whatever happens is the only thing that could have. I learned this from author Bruce Eckel, as one of the rules for open space events.'**

Driscoll: How did you end up co-founding the Brazilian Python Association?

Ramalho: The Brazilian Python community grew organically around a couple of mailing lists and a wiki created by Osvaldo Santana. I was already using Python as my main language, and I had written a tutorial for a magazine, but it was Osvaldo's wiki that encouraged me to engage with the wider community.

Many of us would get together every year at FISL, which was the largest FOSS conference in Brazil. It's incredible how meeting face-to-face, and going out for beers, can strengthen a community that started online.

> **Luciano Ramalho: 'It's incredible how meeting face-to-face, and going out for beers, can strengthen a community that started online.'**

Rodrigo Senra organized the first Brazilian Python conference, and Jean Ferri the second. Running those conferences without a formal support entity was difficult: the organizers couldn't sign contracts, issue invoices, or collect sponsorships in the name of a vague community. So at one FISL, we decided to create the Brazilian Python Foundation.

We faced months of bureaucracy when we learned that foundation is a reserved word under Brazilian law. In order to be a foundation, we needed a five-year plan of action. We needed some staff and an endowment large enough to fund our staff and all of our plans for at least five years. So we had to change our plans and become the more humble Brazilian Python Association (APyB)!

In the end, we succeeded due to our perseverance and the resourcefulness of Dorneles Tremea, our first managing director and my successor as president of the APyB.

Driscoll: I've heard some people challenge the value of APyB. What's your response to such criticism?

Ramalho: Yes, I know that some people have questioned the usefulness of APyB, which does demand some time from its volunteer president and directors after all. My main argument in the defense of APyB is that we tried doing without it and it was worse.

Driscoll: So what open source projects are you working on right now?

Ramalho: Actually, none at this time! I did start the `pingo` project, which is a device-independent API for programming devices with GPIO interfaces. But I only managed to attract Lucas Vido as a solid contributor. Both of us got busy with other things, so the project is abandoned right now. I'd like to reboot it, but I don't know when I'll be able to do that.

All of the code and slides from my conference talks and tutorials is open content. I have over 50 presentations shared for anyone who wants to see them: `https://speakerdeck.com/ramalho`. All of these talks are also on GitHub in the `/fluentpython organization` and in my personal GitHub account (`/ramalho`.)

I've started writing open content for learning Go. It's more likely that my next open source project will be a book or some other content, rather than applications or libraries.

Driscoll: Oh, that's great that you're thinking about writing another book! So do you have any advice for aspiring authors?

Ramalho: Well, I'm no economist, but I think that writing books is just as likely to pay your bills as playing the guitar, so don't do it for the money, but for the love of your subject.

Also, be ready for a very long journey. Have savings, so you can take some time off just to write if needed. Two very successful authors that I know have told me that most of the experiences that they have had with co-authors were bad. So I guess there's no easy way out of the long and mostly lonely journey of being an author!

Driscoll: Have you considered self-publishing at all?

Ramalho: Yes, I have, but while there are several self-publishing alternatives, I think that it's worthwhile to do at least your first book with a good publisher if you can. The first reason is all of the support that you get from a good editor and your technical reviewers. The second reason is the recognition that you get from having a well-known brand promoting your work and adorning its cover.

Driscoll: When you're writing a book, do you create the code before you start writing or not?

Ramalho: I believe that code examples are the heart of any programming book: you can't have an excellent book without excellent examples. David Geary, the author of the classic *Graphic Java* books, once wrote that writing a programming book is essentially coming up with enlightening examples, then surrounding them with explanations. I took his advice and it worked very well for me.

> **Luciano Ramalho: 'I believe that code examples are the heart of any programming book: you can't have an excellent book without excellent examples.'**

So while the hardest part for me is certainly coming up with the examples, I had created a lot of the code before I started writing. I definitely didn't start with an empty text file and a blank screen!

Many of the examples and explanations that are in *Fluent Python* are ones that I'd developed over more than 10 years of teaching and speaking about Python. I did also create many more specifically for the book, and in fact many examples that I never used in the book, because they either became too complicated, or I had then thought of better examples.

> **Luciano Ramalho: 'Here is a great learning point for all Python teachers: we must learn to let go of our examples and writing.'**

Here is a great learning point for all Python teachers: we must learn to let go of our examples and writing, when necessary, no matter how much work we've put into them. So when, as teachers and authors, we find a better approach, or we realize that we've just gone too far, then it's important that we let go of our examples and move on for our readers.

I know already that I will try to drop even more material like this when I work on my next book. I also think about this as a teacher. The writer and aviator Antoine de Saint-Exupéry said in the context of airplane design: "It seems that perfection is attained not when there is nothing more to add, but when there is nothing more to remove."

Driscoll: What are you most excited about in Python today?

Ramalho: Besides the runaway success of Python in data science, I am also excited about the potential of the `async/await` keywords to enable asynchronous programming, not only through the standard `asyncio` library, but also through third-party libraries such as Trio.

Regarding Python 3.7, the addition that most excites me is PEP 557, which introduces a standard way of creating classes with explicit data attributes. This is something that libraries such as ORMs had to reinvent repeatedly.

Driscoll: What do you think about Python 2.7? Should people move to the latest version?

Ramalho: Yes, people should totally move over to Python 3.6. The language is evolving nicely and most libraries have been ported for years now. However, not everyone can afford to make the move.

> **Luciano Ramalho: 'Yes, people should totally move over to Python 3.6. The language is evolving nicely and most libraries have been ported for years now.'**

The trickiest part is sorting out the issue with `strings` versus `bytes`. This is a very positive change, but one that can't be automated, because in Python 2.7 `strings` are sometimes handled as human text and sometimes as `raw bytes`.

Driscoll: What changes would you like to see in future Python releases?

Ramalho: I'd like to see the Global Interpreter Lock (GIL) gone, so that we could leverage all processor cores when using `threads` for CPU intensive work. Unfortunately, the latest effort to do so, by Larry Hastings, seems to have stalled in mid-2017.

The main problem is that removing the GIL would break most (or all, depending on who you ask) external libraries that rely on the Python/C API. One fact that most people don't realize is that without the GIL, writing an extension for Python in another language would be much more complicated. So, although we wish that the GIL did not exist, in reality it is a cornerstone of the success of Python.

Eric Snow, a Python core developer, wrote that the GIL is more of a PR issue. Yes, it is possible to write highly concurrent I/O-bound code using Python `threads` or asynchronous libraries. But when such a project grows, or is heavily stressed, CPU-intensive bottlenecks emerge. Those bottlenecks are extremely hard to find in threaded code, but they slow down everything because of the GIL.

Maybe only a fraction of Python projects is seriously affected by the GIL today, but CPUs are getting more cores and not getting faster, so leveraging multiple cores is becoming more and more important (`https://mail.python.org/pipermail/python-ideas/2015-June/034177.html` or `https://lwn.net/Articles/650521/`).

Driscoll: Thank you, Luciano Ramalho.

18

NICK COGHLAN

Nick Coghlan is an Australian software developer and systems architect. His past roles include software engineer at Boeing Australia and senior software engineer at Red Hat Asia Pacific, a provider of open source solutions. Nick is a CPython core developer and BDFL-delegate for Python packaging interoperability standards. He is a founding member of the Python Software Foundation (PSF)'s Python Packaging Working Group, and the founder of the PyCon Australia Education Seminar. Over the past 20 years, Nick has contributed to a range of open source systems and software projects.

Photo credits of Nick Coghlan: © Kushal Das

Discussion themes: core developers, PEPs, learning Python.

Catch up with Nick Coghlan here: @ncoghlan_dev

Mike Driscoll: What made you decide to become a computer programmer?

Nick Coghlan: Originally, I just did programming as a plaything as a kid. We had the good old BASIC programming book for the Apple IIe.

It wasn't until I did IT in my first year of high school that I discovered that computers were actually a thing you could play with as a job. The school that I went to was one of the first in the state to actually have an IT class. So that was pretty much why I then went into computer systems engineering at university.

My initial full-time job out of university was embedded systems programming in C, for a Texas Instruments DSP. From there, I ended up doing a lot more systems control and automation stuff, which looks a lot more like programming than it does embedded software development. So it was just the case that I enjoyed programming, I was good at it, and you can make money from it.

Driscoll: So why did you move into Python?

Coghlan: So the way that I came to Python is actually kind of interesting, because I was originally a C/C++ developer.

> **Nick Coghlan: 'I was the guy who then replied, "Can we use a different language instead? I already know Java, and I'd like to use Java."'**

My only exposure to Python at university was from a networking lecturer who said, "I'm going to make you all do the assignments in Python, because I'm confident that none of you will know it". I was the guy who then replied, "Can we use a different language instead? I already know Java, and I'd like to use Java".

My lecturer said, "Well, if you really want to use Java then use it, but try Python first". So I tried Python 1.5.2 and it was fun.

Professionally, I was working for a large-scale system integrator here in Australia. For the DSP program I was working on, my test suite was a really rudimentary C program, which was a success if it got to the end without crashing.

We were just having lots of problems with the DSP code not working properly when we got to the next level of integration testing. So we had a huge amount of behavioral bugs getting through. We decided that we needed to write a better test suite to feed the audio in. It was important to check that we were getting the answers we were expecting from the actual data analysis, not simply that we could talk to the DSP and ask it to do things remotely.

> **Nick Coghlan: 'It was important to check that we were getting the answers we were expecting from the actual data analysis.'**

We wanted to check the actual signal processing itself. We also really didn't want to write that in C and C++. Another part of the system had already had Python approved as a language for system control components. So Python wasn't being used for critical path stuff, but just orchestrating all the different bits of the system, and starting them when they were supposed to be started.

There were two main options that we were looking at for doing the automated testing. One option was using Python's `unittest` module, with SWIG, to generate the bindings to the C++ drivers that actually talked to the DSP. The alternative was the in-house C/C++ test framework that we used for everything else. We selected Python.

Driscoll: Why did you choose Python?

Coghlan: The thing was that Python had the `unittest` module to actually organize the testing. Python had SWIG to tie to the C++ driver. We controlled the API of that driver, so making it play nicely with SWIG was straightforward.

Then the last key piece was that Python, in its standard library, had the wave module, to play WAV files out of the PC. So that established a trend for that whole project, which was Australia's High Frequency Modernization Project. Python just ended up kind of proliferating through that project for all of the bits that were testing, mocking and simulating system interfaces for testing purposes.

Driscoll: So I know that another Australian helped to create pywin32. Did you have any involvement in that project?

Coghlan: No, I've only ever been a pywin32 user. There are actually lots of Australians who have historically contributed to the Python community. But because they haven't really been active in PyCon Australia, or anything like that, I've never actually met them!

Driscoll: Well, let's move on. How did you become a core developer for the Python language?

Coghlan: So my short answer to this question is that I became a core developer by arguing with Guido van Rossum!

> **Nick Coghlan: 'I became a core developer by arguing with Guido van Rossum!'**

What actually happened was that I'd been on Usenet since the late 1990s, and so I was very familiar with that whole online discussion format. After I started using Python, I ended up joining the original Python mailing list, and participating in discussions there.

I discovered that Python-Dev was a thing and started lurking on that, originally with the intention just to listen to what people were talking about. I actually started participating actively in discussions and posting as well. The first contribution that I can remember actually making was in discussions on the Python list.

It was very common to use the `timeit` module to time snippets of code and say, "Oh this is faster than that." At that point, if you wanted to time the snippets between two different versions, you had to find where the `timeit` module was in a particular version of the standard library.

We said, "Hang on! Python already knows where the `timeit` module is. Why are we having to tell Python where to find it?" So that ended up becoming a patch to add the initial version of the -m switch in Python 2.4. I think Raymond Hettinger reviewed that. This initial version of Python could only do top-level modules and couldn't do packages or submodules. Then finally by the time we reached Python 2.7, the -m switch actually worked properly and did all the things you would expect of it.

> **Nick Coghlan: 'Finally by the time we reached Python 2.7, the -m switch actually worked properly.'**

Something else interesting happened in late 2004. After a major crunch period at work, I took a leave of absence of three months. I ended up helping out Raymond and Facundo Batista with the initial performance enhancements on the Python decimal module. We were looking at what we could do to make the module faster.

Driscoll: Did you find a way to speed things up?

Coghlan: There was actually an eventual solution several years later, but in those early days, there was lots of benchmarking to say, "How fast can we make this just as a pure Python thing?"

> **Nick Coghlan: 'There was lots of benchmarking to say, "How fast can we make this just as a pure Python thing?"'**

There was a glorious hack that I remember from those days. We made the discovery that in pure Python, if you have a tuple of digits that you would like to turn into a decimal number, then the fastest conversion mechanism that CPython itself offers is to convert all the digits to strings, concatenate the strings, and then use `int` to convert the concatenated string back to a number.

This is because the string `int` conversions have been optimized to a point where doing that is faster than doing all the multiplication and addition operations as Python code. In C, of course, you do the arithmetic. Our findings really annoyed the PyPy developers. From their point of view, doing the arithmetic was a lot better, because the JIT worked. So this meant that their `decimal` module was slower than they liked.

I think that I began getting involved in discussions just after Python 2.3 came out. One of the popular pastimes was making fun of the extended slice syntax. You had the reverse smiley of open bracket, colon, colon, -1, and close bracket, to reverse a sequence. This was long before `reversed` or anything like that.

`reversed` became a thing because it turned out that getting the arithmetic right for reversing a slice was actually quite tricky. It was just really prone to off-by-one errors if you did it manually. So adding in reversed made things easier to read.

Driscoll: What do you think about the long life of Python 2.7? Should people move over to the latest version?

Coghlan: We deliberately set the support period of Python 2.7 such that existing users could make their own decision about when they considered the Python 3 ecosystem to be sufficiently mature for them to switch over.

> **Nick Coghlan: 'We deliberately set the support period of Python 2.7 such that existing users could make their own decision.'**

Folks that had personally felt the pain of Python 2.7's limitations migrated early, so we're now at the point where most of the folks that are still to migrate are either looking for better tools to help them with that process, or are simply planning to sunset affected projects and products along with Python 2.7.

On the tooling front, one of the important use cases for Python 3's type hinting machinery is to allow folks to statically check for Python 3 type correctness errors, even if their automated test coverage is low. This greatly expands the scope of code which can be reliably migrated.

Driscoll: What changes would you like to see in future Python releases?

Coghlan: I'd like to see better tools for working with partially structured hierarchical data, but in a way that preserves Python's reputation as executable pseudo code. I'd also like to continue reducing the discrepancies between what can be done with extension modules, and what specifically requires a Python source module.

Finally, I'd like to see better support for protected memory management models, where rather than aiming to serve as a security boundary, we're instead providing memory separation as a way to assist with maintaining the correctness of concurrent code. CPython's subinterpreter feature already provides this to some degree, but that capability currently has a lot of usability challenges, which Eric Snow is looking to address.

Driscoll: Well good! So let's pretend that I want to become a core developer like you. What would I need to do to actually become one?

Coghlan: So one of the most important things is to figure out why you want to become a core developer. You need the answer to that question because there are going to be inevitable frustrations where you ask yourself: "Why the hell am I doing this?!"

If you don't know what your motivations are, then that's going to be a problem! Nobody else can answer the question for you. Having got past that point, the main thing about becoming a core developer is that a lot of it's actually about trust and earning trust.

> **Nick Coghlan: 'The main thing about becoming a core developer is that a lot of it's actually about trust and earning trust.'**

It's a case of contributing, so as core reviewers we're basically there saying, "Do we want to accept this change and maintain it into the future? Can we give a good answer about why we have accepted the change, if later asked?"

What we're looking for when nominating new core developers and core reviewers is someone whose ability we trust to make good judgements. We want them to say, "Yes, this is a suitable change that will, on balance, make life better for future Python users."

Programming language design is a game of trade-offs. If you try to optimize for everything at once, then you end up optimizing for nothing. So there are a lot of things that have emerged over time as the trade-offs that make something Pythonic. It becomes a matter of understanding whether you can decide something on your own, or whether you need to take a problem to Python-Dev for discussion.

> **Nick Coghlan: 'Programming language design is a game of trade-offs. If you try to optimize for everything at once, then you end up optimizing for nothing.'**

Then there is a final level of escalation, when we say, "This proposal is tricky enough and there are enough subtleties here. There is enough potential controversy here that we should escalate this problem to become a full Python Enhancement Proposal and thrash out the details, before doing anything else." It's ultimately a core developer that makes the decision about where in that spectrum a particular change lies.

> **Nick Coghlan: 'It's ultimately a core developer that makes the decision about where in that spectrum a particular change lies.'**

Driscoll: How does a core developer go about making that decision?

Coghlan: Well, bug fixes are usually pretty straightforward because we know something is wrong. Even with a bug fix though, it's sometimes confusing.

We have three sources of truth, because we have what the reference interpreter does, what the test suite says it does, and what the documentation says it does. When all three of those are in agreement, then you know that there is consistency with what you are doing.

Where things start becoming more of a matter of design judgment is when the interpreter does something, and the test suite and the docs are silent on it. That case just isn't tested, and isn't documented as doing anything in particular. Then the other case is when the documentation says one thing, but the tests and the implementation say something different. In those cases, you have to say, "Well, is the documentation right and it's a bug, or are the docs just wrong?"

Those are the kinds of things that you get to do as a core developer. Whereas when you're contributor, you just want to get your ideas in. That's still a question of trust management, but what you're trying to do is persuade reviewers that your change is worth making. So yeah, it's certainly interesting!

You need to understand what becoming a core developer entails, and why it's something you want. In terms of the practical mechanics of the role, there's the Dev Guide that Brett Cannon originally wrote with BSF funding. The Dev Guide has been maintained and enhanced over time and it explains the difference between being a core developer and being a contributor to CPython.

> **Nick Coghlan: 'There are extra responsibilities that come with being a core developer.'**

There are extra responsibilities that come with being a core developer. The role includes working with issues, working with the reviewer, understanding the review process, discussing things on the mailing lists and making design decisions. You end up dealing with the inevitable frustrations of actually working on such a big project. The core mentorship mailing list can also be useful, depending on the kind of person you are.

Driscoll: So I've always been interested in Python Enhancement Proposals. Could you describe the process of how they get created and accepted?

Coghlan: Yes, so there are two different flows that the Python Enhancement Proposals (PEPs) can go through.

> **Nick Coghlan: 'One flow is when a core developer proposes a change that we know we want to make, but we also know that this change will be big and complex.'**

One flow is when a core developer proposes a change that we know we want to make, but we also know that this change will be big and complex. We know without anybody telling us that this change needs to be a PEP. So in those cases, we'll often just start by writing the PEP and committing the PEP to the PEPs repo.

We will then start the discussion on Python-ideas by saying, "Hey, I've written a new PEP proposing this, and here is why." Discussions basically just start at that level. Core developers manage the PEP process, because we've been through it a few times and we know when a change is big enough to qualify.

For other PEPs, the usual point of genesis is when somebody comes to Python-ideas with a suggestion. This suggestion will have been kicked around as a Python-ideas thread for a bit. People will then have said, "You know what, this actually sounds like it could potentially be a good idea!" The decision is then made to turn the idea into a full PEP and propose the idea that way, rather than just submitting it as an issue on the issue tracker.

That does actually remind me of the third way that PEPs happen. They can come out of discussions on the issue tracker when we definitely know we want to make a change, but there are lots of niggly details. We write a PEP, thrash out the details, and then use that to drive how we implement the idea.

> **Nick Coghlan: 'We write a PEP, thrash out the details, and then use that to drive how we implement the idea.'**

Driscoll: So are these changes just discussed until they eventually get ironed out, and then accepted or rejected?

Coghlan: It depends on the proposal. With some proposals, the change itself is not controversial, but the details just need thrashing out.

Those proposals will usually go through some discussion on Python-ideas and Python-Dev. The decision will then be made to stop thrashing out the idea and start implementing it. The proposal becomes an accepted PEP and eventually goes through to final.

Some proposals are more borderline and we put a question to Python-Dev about whether they are in fact a good idea. We do actually have a proposal open at the moment around the null coalescing operator. We genuinely don't know if we want to proceed. This PEP would make the language more complex, because it's a cryptic syntax that people would have to learn and understand. So that's the main argument against the idea. But on the argument in favor, you're saying, "Well, this is a pattern that comes up fairly often in data manipulation pipelines."

So that PEP is still in discussion, until it does get to the point of finally being put to Python-Dev as a yes or no question. Then the decision will be made that yes we definitely want to proceed, or no we don't, unless something changes.

> **Nick Coghlan: 'Very occasionally, you do get PEPs that are written specifically to be rejected.'**

Very occasionally, you do get PEPs that are written specifically to be rejected. In those cases, an idea keeps coming up, but the arguments against it have never been clearly documented anywhere. So someone is just taking the time to write down the idea and write down all the reasons that we rejected the PEP, before saying, "Right! I'm posting this as a rejected PEP, to say this is why we don't do this". That makes me think of some of the new stuff that I've seen in Python 3.5 and 3.6, that was only partially accepted and classed as provisional.

Driscoll: So is that slightly different? Does that mean that people have agreed enough that they want to add something, but they may not keep it?

Coghlan: Yes, so we got caught a couple of times when we accepted a change, and the new API, and immediately put it under our standard backwards compatibility guarantee.

What we ended up doing was painting ourselves into a corner. We were stuck supporting an API that actually wasn't very good for the problem it was aiming to solve. We were getting these suggestions and potential module additions that were clearly beneficial and clearly helpful for users. The problem was that we were not sure we had the API design details right.

> **Nick Coghlan: 'We were stuck supporting an API that actually wasn't very good for the problem it was aiming to solve.'**

We didn't want to put anything under our full standard library backwards compatibility guarantee, so we decided not to include the additions. This approach ended up being bad for everyone, because it kept things out of the standard library that really should have been in there.

We also couldn't use that type of module to help us to improve other parts of the standard library. Honestly, one of the main ways that new building blocks get into the standard library is because we want to use them in other parts of the standard library. So there's a standard library `enum` type now, because we wanted `enum` types in things like the socket module.

The provisional PEP, which I think ended up being PEP 411, went through a few iterations. Basically PEP 411 was designed to give us that ability to accept modules that we're pretty confident we're going to keep, but we're not sure we have the API design details right yet.

We leave a PEP as provisional for a couple of releases, to give ourselves the right to make breaking changes to the API if we mess something up. I think async I/O only just went non-provisional in Python 3.6.

> **Nick Coghlan: 'We leave a PEP as provisional for a couple of releases, to give ourselves the right to make breaking changes to the API if we mess something up.'**

Driscoll: So does leaving a PEP as provisional work well?

Coghlan: Yes, we're actually really happy with how that's worked out. It lets us give people that clear warning that a PEP is still a bit in flux. This lets users know that we're still figuring out the details and if this bothers them, then they shouldn't use that PEP yet.

There was actually an interesting example recently for Python 3.6 with `pathlib`. So `pathlib` had been included as a provisional API and it had lots of interoperability problems with other standard library APIs that were expecting strings.

> **Nick Coghlan: 'For Python 3.6, pathlib had hit a crossroads.'**

For Python 3.6, `pathlib` had hit a crossroads and was either going to get taken out of the standard library again and pushed back to purely being a PyPI module, or the interoperability issues had to be fixed. That was the either/or decision that was before the core development team for Python 3.6.

This decision became the `os.path` protocol, or the `os.fspath` protocol and the path-like objects support, which is basically fixing the interoperability problem for `pathlib`. So this means that there are a lot of standard library APIs now that automatically accept path-like objects.

Driscoll: Alright, so what is the Python Packaging Authority?

Coghlan: So the Python Packaging Authority's name actually started as a joke by the pip and virtualenv developers. They wanted a name for the development team that covered both projects. So they said, "Let's call ourselves the Python Packaging Authority, because nobody expects the Python Packaging Authority!"

Then, back in 2013, we were starting to actively try to bring more of the tools, like `setuptools` and `distutils`, into that space. The Python Packaging User Guide started bringing all that information together, to offer a more coherent and officially recommended way of doing things. We needed a name for that umbrella group too. We decided that the Python Packaging Authority was kind of cool as a name, so we could start bringing in more projects under that umbrella.

> **Nick Coghlan: 'We decided that the Python Packaging Authority was kind of cool as a name, so we could start bringing in more projects under that umbrella.'**

Basically, the Python Packaging Authority occupies a role around packaging tools and interoperability standards, that's similar to the role that core developers play in relation to Python as a whole. While there's some overlap between people who are interested in programming language design and people who are interested in software distribution design, there are a lot of people who fall on one side or the other. Those people aren't the least bit interested in the other aspects.

Separating the two types of people means that anyone who cares about both types of design can participate in both subcommunities. But we're not constantly trying to explain the complexities of software distribution to language designers and vice versa. I think this split has made people a lot happier in general. It's nice to be in a group that you understand. I like packaging, but I like Python too. So I'm kind of torn on which one I'd probably fall under. I'd probably want to work on Python and the Python Packaging Authority too.

> **Nick Coghlan: 'I like packaging, but I like Python too. So I'm kind of torn on which one I'd probably fall under.'**

Driscoll: Python is one of the major languages being used in AI and machine learning. Why do you think this is?

Coghlan: AI and machine learning are an interesting mix of exploratory interactive data analysis and heavy-duty number-crunching. CPython's rich C API has led to Python serving as a 'glue' language for interconnecting high performance components written in languages like C, C++, and Fortran.

The scientific research community has been using Python that way for more than 20 years (the first version of Numeric was released in 1995). This means that Python offers a unique hybrid of a flexible, yet easy-to-learn and general-purpose computing language, combined with a set of scientific computing libraries, developed for use in high-performance computing environments.

Driscoll: What could be done to make Python a better language for AI and machine learning?

Coghlan: On the ease of use side, there are still a lot of opportunities to make components more readily available to users, either through preconfigured freemium web services (like Google Colabatory or Microsoft Azure Notebooks), or locally through the Python and Conda packaging toolchains.

On the performance side, there are also a lot of unexplored opportunities to better optimize the CPython interpreter and the Cython static compiler (for example, Cython doesn't currently ship a shared dynamic runtime, so there's likely a lot of duplicated boilerplate code in generated modules, that not only makes them larger and slower to compile, but also slower to import at runtime).

Driscoll: So I noticed that you are a fellow blogger. How long have you been writing about Python and what made you decide to become a blogger?

Coghlan: It was probably around Python 3.3 that I started talking about programming stuff on my blog. Mostly, I find writing is a very useful aid to thinking. You're forced to get an idea coherent enough to be readable. So that's mainly the way that I still use the blog now. If there's something in particular about Python that I want to reference later, then I write down my current thoughts.

Driscoll: In your opinion, is Python a good language to actually start learning programming with?

Coghlan: I do recommend Python as a first text-based language. For a lot of people, starting with one of the plug-and-play languages is a good alternative if they want to get the basic concepts down.

> **Nick Coghlan: 'Once you want to get into full combinatorial programming, then Python's a very good language.'**

Once you want to get into full combinatorial programming, then Python's a very good language. The deliberate language design restrictions are not very bright. You cannot get them to parse very complicated action at a distance things. If you study linguistics, then you realize that the human brain also struggles to parse complicated at a distance things.

So the advantage of Python is that you only need one token look ahead to understand the context of the thing you're currently looking at. You don't need to keep much in your head to understand what the code is trying to tell you. We try to keep things visible as to where different names are coming from. I think that makes a surprising amount of difference to how easy it is for people to fit ideas into their brain.

I made a post several years ago about scripting languages and suitable complexity. If you look at a cookbook, or a work instruction guide, then you will find procedural instructions. The outer layer of a cookbook is very much procedural and sequential. Then the subfunctions and the objects are all kind of embedded within that framework. I think Python works well for people because it reflects how we interact with the world.

> **Nick Coghlan: 'I think Python works well for people because it reflects how we interact with the world.'**

Driscoll: Could you explain a little more about why Python works so well?

Coghlan: Sure, we do things in sequence. Starting procedurally as your foundation, and then layering all of your other things on top, as you need them, makes a lot of sense.

Object-oriented programming, functional programming and event-based programming are all techniques that we have come up with to manage complexity. Whichever one of them you choose, as your fundamental organizing principle for your language, then sets the minimum level of complexity for what you do.

It's really interesting to talk to people that teach with robotics and the embodied computing type environment. When you teach that way, starting with objects is a good way to go. Embodied computing people have that natural ability to say, "That robot sitting on my desk corresponds to the class 'Robot' in my program." They can do that visual correlation.

I think it's the case that procedural by default really does match the way cookbooks and instructions are written. That is good for lowering barriers to entry but, at the same time, Python is a language that can grow with you. Python has all the tools to do mathematical programming, object-oriented programming and functional programming.

> **Nick Coghlan: 'Python is a language that can grow with you.'**

You can use Python based on the kinds of problems that you have. When you start learning more about particular aspects of Python, then you can use that as a launching point to get into languages that specialize in a particular area. So you can use Python to launch into Haskell (functional programming), Java or C#.

Driscoll: So let's pretend that I know all the basics of Python and now I want to enhance my understanding of the language. What should I do?

Coghlan: The important question to ask yourself at this point is how you learn. So for example, for myself, I figured out that I'm very much about needs-based learning.

> **Nick Coghlan: 'I learned new programming techniques and new libraries in order to solve a problem.'**

I don't do well learning things just for the sake of learning them. I learn new programming techniques and new libraries in order to solve a problem. In my case, I find the problem I'm interested in solving and then learn whatever I need to do to solve that.

In terms of learning more, Allison Kaptur has written some quite good stuff. We've started adding a section to the Dev Guide about diving into internals. One useful trick can be to look at something you use every day, particularly an open source library, and just start digging into the code.

> **Nick Coghlan: 'Look at something you use every day, particularly an open source library, and just start digging into the code.'**

So in the standard library, there will actually be links to the source code from the standard library module documentation. Actually just going and reading that, and trying to figure out why certain things are done, can be useful.

That reminds me of another interesting project called Python Tutor (pythontutor.com). Python Tutor is a code visualizer or a behavioral visualizer. As you work through the code, Python Tutor has a little system model that it updates progressively, explaining what's going on.

One strategy, that I know some people have certainly found useful, is trying to change things, not because they actually want to make a change, but just to learn the mechanics of what's involved.

Driscoll: What are you most excited about in Python today?

Coghlan: I'll give a split answer here, as my professional and personal perspectives on the question are slightly different.

In a lot of ways, Python has done to the Linux ecosystem what the Linux ecosystem did to enterprise organizations in general: become ubiquitous without anyone really bothering to tell executive management about it. This means that everything we've achieved so far has been done primarily through the efforts of the volunteer community contributors, with only occasional and intermittent investments from large commercial and institutional users.

> **Nick Coghlan: 'Everything we've achieved so far has been done primarily through the efforts of the volunteer community contributors.'**

So professionally, the thing that most excites me is the fact that the increase in the use of AI and machine learning techniques in business software development is prompting a lot of organizations to realize that there's more to the world of software development than the current enterprise incumbents of C, C++, Java, and C#.

This has been most clearly visible in recent years through IEEE Spectrum's annual multi-data-source language ranking, where Python started out, in 2014, at the edge of the top five (with C#), but has steadily climbed through those rankings, reaching first place in the 2017 edition of the survey.

Personally, the thing that most excites me is the way we're getting teachers and other educators directly involved in the open source Python community. Prompted by an excellent keynote from James Curran at PyCon Australia 2014, and the Education Track at PyCon UK, I founded the PyCon Australia Education Seminar in 2015, and we've been running that every year since.

A lot of Python user groups also have a specific focus on adult education and offer workshops for folks either looking to improve their computing skills in their current profession, or contemplating a career change into software development.

Driscoll: Thank you, Nick Coghlan.

19

MIKE BAYER

Mike Bayer is an American software developer and a senior software engineer at Red Hat, which sells open source software products. Previous positions include many New York-based internet companies like MLB.com. He also worked on content management software at Major League Baseball. Mike is the creator of a number of open source programming libraries for Python, such as SQLAlchemy, an SQL toolkit and object-relational mapper. He plays an active role in the Python community by promoting good database software practices. Mike is a regular speaker at PyCon US and smaller conferences in Europe.

Discussion themes: SQLAlchemy, AI, v2.7/v3.x.
Catch up with Mike Bayer here: @zzzeek

Mike Driscoll: What made you become a programmer?

Mike Bayer: I've had an interest in computers since 1980, when I was first exposed to early personal computers. I tried to learn game programming in assembly language for early 8-bit computers, without much success. In high school, I was exposed to data structures and procedural programming with Pascal.

It seemed pretty natural that I'd become a programmer, but as it turned out, I switched majors from computer engineering to music and took several years off from touching computers at all. I had found myself being overly competitive with other programmers that I met on bulletin boards and I didn't like who I was.

I got back into computers strictly because it was the only way that I could eat and pay rent. About that time, the internet became a commercial industry and I immediately got involved in that kind of work.

Once the first internet bubble came along, being a programmer in NYC was suddenly intense and exciting. Everyone wanted you to work for them. The competitive element of programming has in fact created continuous problems for me over the years. I've had to work to minimize that issue.

Driscoll: So how did you get started with Python?

Bayer: Most of my pre-Python career was spent programming in Perl, Java, and a little bit of C. I was really into object-oriented application design and I ended up going through a deep architecture astronaut phase, which was very common with Java programmers in the late 1990s and early 2000s.

I liked the idea of scripting languages, because they allowed you to jump right into a text file. You would have something that could work immediately without the formality, boilerplate and compilation step of Java. So I also spent a lot of time trying to realize OO design in Perl, which was pretty unsatisfying.

> **Mike Bayer: 'After a few years of refusing to accept significant whitespace, I finally got into Python.'**

I became aware that Python might be something that could really strike a balance between those two worlds. After a few years of refusing to accept significant whitespace, I finally got into Python and realized that the language was in fact everything that I was looking for.

Mike Driscoll: What makes Python special to you?

Bayer: What impressed me about Python was the way that everything in your interpreter was a Python object, including all of the modules that you imported.

Nowadays, that whole way of looking at things is second nature to me. But when I first learned that I could inspect elements of the program itself as just more data, all of the other languages that I'd been exposed to were nothing like that.

Python was so simple to understand, especially after I had spent years never really understanding what Perl's use statement did. I also observed in Python a certain emphasis on consistency and correctness that was uncharacteristic in scripting languages in general.

I predicted that the Python programmers that I'd be working with would be higher quality developers than I'd otherwise been exposed to, since they were attracted to Python! That turned out to be completely true.

Driscoll: So what inspired you to create SQLAlchemy?

Bayer: Well, I had always had the goal of figuring out which programming language I wanted to make my home in. Within that language, I wanted to work up a full suite of tools that I could use for everything. I wanted to be able to strike out independently and build applications for people.

> **Mike Bayer: 'I wanted to be able to strike out independently and build applications for people.'**

At my various jobs, I had always had to create some kind of database abstraction layer that I'd then use in many projects. I was always building little template engines, mini web frameworks and database abstraction layers, in whatever language I was using, which I'd try to standardize for all of my projects.

So when I got into Python, I was unsatisfied with the web framework tools and database abstraction tools that were available at that time. I had also written many template engines and database access tools already, so I had a lot of ideas.

> **Mike Bayer: 'When I got into Python, I was unsatisfied with the web framework tools and database abstraction tools that were available at that time.'**

I first wrote a template engine called Myghty, which was an almost line-for-line port of the Perl template engine HTML::Mason. Myghty was horrible, yet it gained some brief popularity and formed the basis of the first version of the Pylons web framework.

When I set out to write SQLAlchemy, I took a very deep and slow approach, to try to make it amazing. I was still very flawed as a programmer and especially as a Python programmer at that point. Early SQLAlchemy had many awful design choices, but it still shined as something that was truly unique and potentially kind of amazing. The first time that I saw the unit of work do a flush, I was amazed. I realized that this thing might have a deep impact on people.

Driscoll: So how did Mako come about?

Bayer: Mako was very simply created to replace Myghty and all of its horrible design choices, so that Pylons could have a template engine that wasn't embarrassing.

Mako was meant to be a very capable and solid template engine, which could more or less be left to go on its own once it was complete. While Mako did gain more features over the years, I've considered it to be complete for many years now. I still use Mako, but I'm happy for Jinja2 to be the de facto template engine in Python. Armin Ronacher did, after all, credit Mako's architecture for being a lot of his inspiration for creating Jinja2.

> **Mike Bayer: 'I still use Mako, but I'm happy for Jinja2 to be the de facto template engine in Python.'**

Driscoll: If you could start over with SQLAlchemy, what would you do differently?

Bayer: There were some mistakes that I made, which led to scenarios that ultimately benefited the project immensely. So if I had not made those mistakes, then I'm not sure how things would have turned out.

My issue with competitiveness, which I've mentioned, caused me to have poor interactions very early on with some of the contributors. Chasing away people who had good ideas, and in many cases, saw things much more clearly than I did, was a huge mistake.

I should also have spent more time reading other Python code and getting better at using the correct idiomatic patterns, rather than having to retroactively fix all of the code once I learned new things about Python.

If I could start over with SQLAlchemy, I would do other things differently too. There were a lot of design patterns that were in the 0.1 version that I tried to get rid of by version 0.2 or 0.3. I couldn't remove those patterns totally.

Version 0.1 relied heavily on the implicit association of objects with database connections, both at the core and ORM levels. Today, two of these patterns still exist as bound metadata and connectionless execution. These patterns remain extremely popular, but continue to create subtle confusion, in contrast to the newer patterns that are based on explicitness.

> **Mike Bayer: 'Had I been starting with what I know today, SQLAlchemy would have been much closer to the mark to begin with.'**

There are many other API patterns that have been heavily revised over the years. Had I been starting with what I know today, then SQLAlchemy would have been much closer to the mark to begin with. There would have been no need to go through major API changes in the early releases.

I also should have recognized the need for a good SQL migrations tool early on, although sqlalchemy-migrate did a good job of handling this until I had time to create Alembic migrations.

Driscoll: What have you learned from creating open source projects?

Bayer: Well, for one thing, if your open source project turns out to be popular, then it will never be finished. If your project is linked to some set of constantly changing technology, like Python database APIs, then your work will never be done.

> **Mike Bayer: 'If your open source project turns out to be popular, then it will never be finished.'**

I had no idea that the pace of bug fixing would remain constant for over ten years. I have also learned that to be successful in open source, you do have to have a lot of luck. You must be fortunate enough to be doing a project at the right time. I got into Python much earlier than most of the community and produced my software at the perfect time.

Finally, I've learned a lot about the calculus that you must apply when a user wants some feature, or behavior X. You can't really take them at their word. Often, when users think that they want X, they really want Y. Sometimes they think that they want X, but they haven't thought through the ramifications.

You always have to be very careful about how you go about adding X. At the same time, you don't want the user to be upset if you are denying their feature request. Above all, as the maintainer, you need to be as courteous as possible. This is extremely difficult, because lots of users are pretty disrespectful and entitled. You gain nothing by venting about this though.

Driscoll: We're seeing Python being used a lot in AI and machine learning. Why do you think that Python is such a great language for this?

Bayer: What we're doing in that field is developing our math and algorithms. We're putting the algorithms that we definitely want to keep and optimize into libraries such as scikit-learn. Then we're continuing to iterate and share notes on how we organize and think about the data.

> **Mike Bayer: 'A high-level scripting language is ideal for AI and machine learning, because we can quickly move things around and try again.'**

A high-level scripting language is ideal for AI and machine learning, because we can quickly move things around and try again. The code that we create spends most of its lines on representing the actual math and data structures, not on boilerplate.

A scripting language like Python is even better, because it is strict and consistent. Everyone can understand each other's Python code much better than they could in some other language that has confusing and inconsistent programming paradigms.

The availability of tools like IPython notebook has made it possible to iterate and share our math and algorithms on a whole new level. Python emphasizes the core of the work that we're trying to do and completely minimizes everything else about how we give the computer instructions, which is how it should be. Automate whatever you don't need to be thinking about.

> **Mike Bayer: 'Automate whatever you don't need to be thinking about.'**

Driscoll: How do you think that Python could be a better language for AI and machine learning?

Bayer: Machine learning is a CPU intensive task, so we need to continue iterating on how to make better use of all of those processor cores, which unfortunately means the Global Interpreter Lock (GIL). Right now, the only way to do that is to use multiprocessing.

> **Mike Bayer: 'Python still lacks a decent concurrency paradigm.'**

Python still lacks a decent concurrency paradigm that is somewhere between threads, where Python's dynamic contract means that we have a GIL and processes, which incur complexity and expense regarding how to share data. It might be helpful to have an interpreter concept that acts largely like multiprocessing, but is somehow doing it within a single process space. This concept would use OS-level threads, yet still keep the processes isolated enough that they don't share the same GIL.

Driscoll: What advice would you give to someone who is new to programming in general?

Bayer: There is a lot of conventional wisdom in computer programming. You should always put conventional wisdom on trial.

> **Mike Bayer: 'You should always put conventional wisdom on trial.'**

There are rules in programming, such as don't use mutable global variables, which are actually more like training wheels for beginners. They are good rules, that have a lot of truth in them, but none of them apply in every case.

As you progress from being a beginner to being more advanced, you want to be able to think on your own. You also want to gain experience by finding novel and creative ways to solve problems. These ideas might not always work out, but establishing a core practice, of always challenging the status quo, will hopefully allow you to see a great new solution to a problem one day.

Driscoll: Which language would you recommend to someone who is starting out in programming?

Bayer: I think Python is the best beginner language that I've ever seen. For your first few years of programming, you can just use Python and you'll probably be doing JavaScript as well, since the browser is unavoidable.

At some point, it's also a great idea to write some kind of scripting language interpreter or compiler. An understanding of how instructions declared at a high level, like a Python function, end up manifesting as instructions run by a CPU, is an essential perspective to have.

Driscoll: What about Python today most excites you?

Bayer: I'm excited that Python is becoming the default language that virtually everyone who wants to do thoughtful work with data chooses first, particularly in the field of journalism.

> **Mike Bayer: 'I look forward to a new crop of journalists who can program Python as well as they can write a headline.'**

Journalism is becoming more data-driven and I look forward to a new crop of journalists who can program Python as well as they can write a headline. We need journalists who can produce stories that are based on data from the ground up. This will hopefully lead to more data being available as the demand increases. Imagine if each time we read a story in the Washington Post, there was also an IPython notebook right there, which we could use to analyze the data in the story.

Driscoll: Should people now leave Python 2.7 behind?

Bayer: Moving from Python 2.7 is a problem that will solve itself. I think that people in the data field are definitely starting with the 3.x series now. In the infrastructure world that I work in, we are understandably taking a lot longer to get there, but we will.

> **Mike Bayer: 'Moving from Python 2.7 is a problem that will solve itself. I think that people in the data field are definitely starting with the 3.x series now.'**

Driscoll: What are some changes that you're hoping to see in future Python releases?

Bayer: To be honest, in the future I'd like to see less emphasis on the `asyncio` system, which I believe is a widely misunderstood API.

New programmers are starting their projects using async for the entire system end-to-end. They are creating buggy and overly complicated applications as a result, which don't perform any better than they would using traditional techniques.

There is definitely a place for asynchronous I/O, but in virtually any real-world application, it should be limited to dealing with interaction with external resources and clients. This should only be when the scale of external data interaction will be very wide and concurrent (e.g. scraping thousands of websites, or waiting for commands from thousands of clients).

The central engines of our applications (those which are interacting with local data and doing our business logic and algorithms), should be written with traditional threading. Asynchronous and synchronous components can talk to each other quite well, however the programmer needs to understand both paradigms well. The current async culture does not emphasize this at all.

Driscoll: Thank you, Mike Bayer.

20

Jake Vanderplas

Jake Vanderplas is a data scientist and the author of *Python Data Science Handbook*. He is a director of open software for the University of Washington's eScience Institute, where he works with researchers from a variety of disciplines. Previous roles at the University of Washington include director of research in physical sciences. Jake is a long-time contributor to the Python scientific stack and has worked on projects such as SciPy, scikit-learn and Altair. He regularly speaks at Python conferences in the US and has delivered keynote speeches at PyCon, PyData and SciPy. Jake is a visiting researcher at Google and writes a tech blog.

Discussion themes: Python in data science and astronomy.

Catch up with Jake Vanderplas here: @jakevd

Mike Driscoll: Could you tell me a little about your background?

Jake Vanderplas: I studied physics as an undergraduate and spent a few years after college working in the outdoors as an environmental educator and a mountaineering guide.

After a few summers sleeping under the stars each night in California's Sierra Nevada, I fell in love with astronomy and decided to take advantage of my physics background to head to graduate school and learn more.

Up until my first year of graduate school, I'd only done a bit of coding. I had messed around with HyperCard in middle school and taken a C++ class in high school. I had also learned some basic Mathematica in college.

Driscoll: How did you get started using the Python programming language?

Vanderplas: Astronomy is very computationally-driven these days and so when I started graduate school, I needed to relearn how to code.

> **Jake Vanderplas: 'Astronomy is very computationally-driven these days...'**

Most of my department was using IDL in those days, but I was lucky enough to do a quarter-long research project with a professor who recommended Python. He told me that Python was the future and in retrospect he was entirely correct!

I taught myself Python over winter break by writing a Sudoku puzzle solver and then turning that into a Sudoku puzzle generator. Much later on, I arrived at PyCon 2017 and explained why Python is liked and used by so many scientists.

Driscoll: What do you like about Python?

Vanderplas: I like Python first of all because it is open, which is a huge advantage over some other tools favored by academics (Mathematica, IDL and MATLAB come to mind).

When I first started using Python, I found the syntax and semantics to be incredibly clean and intuitive, which made coding fun for me in a way that it never was when I was first learning C++.

> **Jake Vanderplas: 'I found Python's syntax and semantics to be incredibly clean and intuitive.'**

Also, the scientific Python ecosystem, even though it was fairly nascent when I started, is a huge boon. No matter what you want to do with Python in science, it's likely that someone has created a package for it.

Python's interoperability with so many other languages means that it can act like the glue between the various tools that scientists need to use together. Then the 'batteries included' aspect of Python means that there's a built-in library for nearly everything and a third-party library for everything else.

> **Jake Vanderplas: 'Python...can act like the glue between the various tools that scientists need to use together.'**

Python's simple and dynamic nature makes it perfect for day-to-day scientific data exploration, where speed of development is primary and speed of execution is often secondary.

Last but not least, Python's open ethos does fit well with science and we're seeing an increasing number of scientists hosting their research code on GitHub and similar services, to aid in reproducibility.

Driscoll: How is Python's open ethos helping the scientific community?

Vanderplas: Python's open ethos is a great match for how science should be done. I made the point in my keynote at PyCon 2017 that over the past five to ten years, scientists have really absorbed many of the best-practice lessons from the open source community.

Code sharing, version control, unit testing, and code documentation are essential for making sure that modern science is reproducible. The people doing the best computational work in the scientific community have adapted many of these practices from the open source (and particularly Python open source) community.

Driscoll: What is Python missing that would be great for scientists?

Vanderplas: The biggest challenge with Python for scientists is that the scaling of computation requires writing code in a language other than Python.

> **Jake Vanderplas: 'The biggest challenge with Python for scientists is that the scaling of computation requires writing code in a language other than Python.'**

Tools like Cython and Numba address part of this problem by letting you convert Python or Python-like code to fast compiled code, but there is a cognitive overhead involved in deciding when and where to switch to these additional tools. PyPy is promising, but the problem is that it doesn't support CPython's C-API, which the bulk of the scientific ecosystem requires.

This is why some people in the community are attracted to Julia. It's a language built for scientific computation, with fast LLVM-based execution built-in from the ground up. That said, Julia feels a bit clunky to me in some areas and I wish we could have a happy medium: Python's syntax with Julia's performance.

Driscoll: How can the Python community help the scientific community to learn Python? What projects are you currently using Python in?

Vanderplas: I do all of my daily work in Python. Currently I'm involved in several research projects at the University of Washington (UW). I'm mentoring students working on astronomy and on transportation-focused data science.

I'm helping to develop the Altair library, which is a Python interface to the Vega-Lite grammar of visualization. I think it will be a good fit for one of the current holes in the Python scientific space, which is exploratory data analysis.

> **Jake Vanderplas: 'I generally push Python... and these days, I rarely have to push very hard!'**

Part of my job at UW is essentially consulting with researchers around the university to help with computational or statistical aspects of their research. I generally push Python in most of those cases and these days, I rarely have to push very hard!

Driscoll: Do most astronomists do a lot of computer programming?

Vanderplas: Computing is absolutely essential in modern astronomy! The field has, for the most part, moved beyond the romantic days of traveling to remote peaks to peer through telescopes. Even when observing on-site, observations are recorded by CCDs attached to the telescopes.

Beyond that, it's generally true that all of the *easy* observations have already been made. To really push forward our understanding of the universe requires novel studies. That novelty might mean observing very faint objects (in which case detailed noise models are a necessity), or observing many objects to learn about their statistical properties (in which a scalable computing environment is essential).

At either end of that spectrum, you better know how to write code to ingest telescope images, model the interesting feature and spit out useful results.

Driscoll: How common is it for scientists to need to write code?

Vanderplas: Like in astronomy, scientists in most fields are finding coding to be essential.

> **Jake Vanderplas: 'Scientists in most fields are finding coding to be essential.'**

We astronomers have been a bit ahead of the curve when it comes to data volumes, but as sensors, cameras, satellites and other devices become cheaper and more abundant, the *data deluge* is starting to be a feature in most other domains as well.

Driscoll: Which scientific fields use programming the most?

Vanderplas: It's very hard to say, but immense volumes of data are being produced in astronomy.

So in radio astronomy, for example, there are projects that are producing data at rates of about 5GB/s. In physics, the LHC produces data at a rate of about 25GB/s. Then in biostatistics, gene sequencing data for an individual is typically ~100s of GB. All of these fields are using sophisticated algorithms to extract meaning from that data.

Driscoll: On the other side of the coin, are you aware of any scientific fields where Python is weak in? If so, what are they?

Vanderplas: Some fields have long histories of ingrained toolchains. For example, MATLAB could probably be described as standard in many engineering and applied math departments.

Ten years ago, a language called IDL dominated most of astronomy research, but that has changed and now Python is the dominant language mentioned in refereed publications.

The way this changed in astronomy was two-fold. You had some visionaries in positions of influence that pushed for Python early on (for example, Perry Greenfield at the Space Telescope Science Institute). Then there was a real groundswell coming from graduate students and postdocs, who worked hard to train each other (examples are software carpentry workshops and the SciCoder program).

> **Jake Vanderplas: 'The momentum of Python sort of took over.'**

There has also been a community-wide push to standardize the astronomy Python tool stack. The result is the (phenomenal) Astropy project. Beyond that, the momentum of Python sort of took over.

Driscoll: Thank you, Jake Vanderplas.

Other Books You May Enjoy

If you enjoyed this book, you may be interested in these other books by Packt:

Python Machine Learning - Second Edition

Sebastian Raschka, Vahid Mirjalili

ISBN: 978-1-78712-593-3

- Understand the key frameworks in data science, machine learning, and deep learning
- Harness the power of the latest Python open source libraries in machine learning
- Master machine learning techniques using challenging real-world data
- Master deep neural network implementation using the TensorFlow library
- Ask new questions of your data through machine learning models and neural networks
- Learn the mechanics of classification algorithms to implement the best tool for the job
- Predict continuous target outcomes using regression analysis
- Uncover hidden patterns and structures in data with clustering
- Delve deeper into textual and social media data using sentiment analysis

Artificial Intelligence with Python

Prateek Joshi

ISBN: 978-1-78646-439-2

- Realize different classification and regression techniques
- Understand the concept of clustering and how to use it to automatically segment data
- See how to build an intelligent recommender system
- Understand logic programming and how to use it
- Build automatic speech recognition systems
- Understand the basics of heuristic search and genetic programming
- Develop games using Artificial Intelligence
- Learn how reinforcement learning works
- Discover how to build intelligent applications centered on images, text, and time series data
- See how to use deep learning algorithms and build applications based on it

Understanding Software

Max Kanat-Alexander

ISBN: 978-1-78862-881-5

- See how to bring simplicity and success to your programming world
- Clues to complexity - and how to build excellent software
- Simplicity and software design
- Principles for programmers
- The secrets of rockstar programmers
- Max's views and interpretation of the Software industry
- Why Programmers suck and how to suck less as a programmer
- Software design in two sentences
- What is a bug? Go deep into debugging

Leave a review - let other readers know what you think

Please share your thoughts on this book with others by leaving a review on the site that you bought it from. If you purchased the book from Amazon, please leave us an honest review on this book's Amazon page. This is vital so that other potential readers can see and use your unbiased opinion to make purchasing decisions, we can understand what our customers think about our products, and our authors can see your feedback on the title that they have worked with Packt to create. It will only take a few minutes of your time, but is valuable to other potential customers, our authors, and Packt. Thank you!

INDEX

C

D

E

F

G

J

K

L

M

N

O

P

Q

R

S

Made in the USA
Coppell, TX
06 June 2020

27138700R00203